London Buses

A Brief History

John Reed

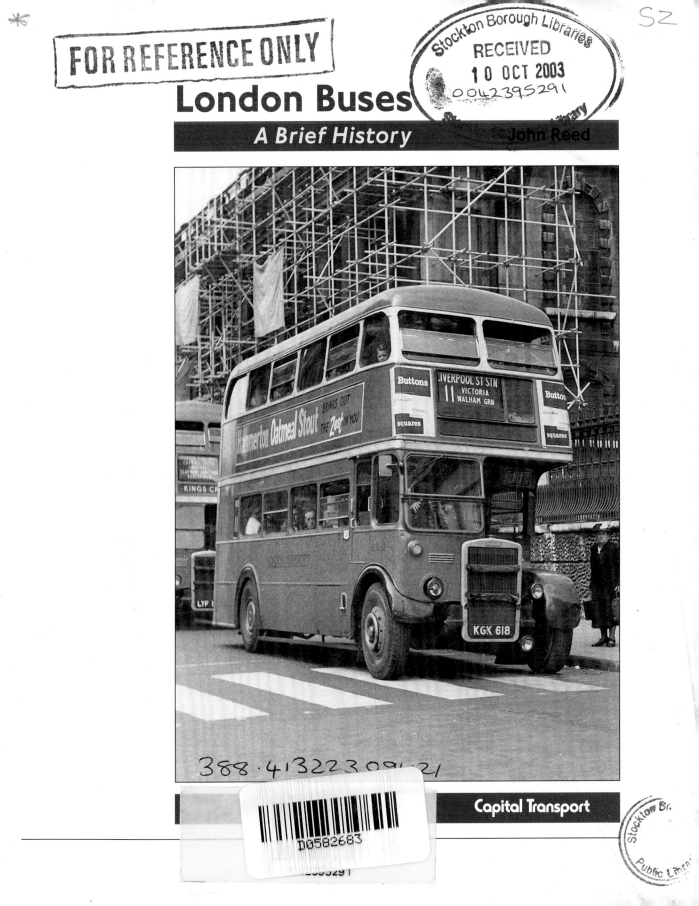

Capital Transport

ISBN 185414 233 X

Published by Capital Transport Publishing
38 Long Elmes, Harrow Weald, Middlesex

Printed by CS Graphics, Singapore

Designed by Tim Demuth

Contents

ISLINGTON SOMERS TOWN

PADDINGTON to the BANK

DIORAMA REGENT'S PARK

OMNIBUS

Nineteenth-Century Beginnings

The first Omnibuses, including Shillibeer's original illustrated here, were fairly primitive despite most having stylish external liveries. Inside there was no lighting or heating, save for straw strewn over the floor in winter to keep feet warm and collect mud brought on to the buses by boots or buckled shoes. Despite these rather base and, in damp weather, unsavoury conditions the new mode of transport soon gained enormous appeal, although for many decades the omnibus was the conveyance of the well-healed middle classes. The Omnibus took up to an hour to travel the length of the route from Paddington to Bank. LT Museum

London is full of landmarks which fill the cities of London and Westminster to the brim. Not just the elegant public buildings but also the shops, the theatres and cinemas, museums and galleries, the markets, the acres and acres of parkland, and the river. Linking them all are London's red buses, threading their way through the streets of commerce and commercialism and out into the suburbs with their supermarkets and semi's.

The story of the London bus goes back to the summer of 1829. A glance around London at that time would reveal countless horse-drawn coaches creaking and lurching through narrow and congested streets. In amongst them would be small one- or two-seater hackney coaches weaving in and out of the general mêlée. The large coaches would be full to bursting, carrying people to and from districts which, by the end of the century, would have been fused together to create the County of London – places like Hackney and Hammersmith, Paddington and Peckham, which in the 1820s were quiet suburbs still somewhat remote from the 'stones', the paved area of London, equivalent to today's City and West End.

The coaches were called 'short stages' and advance booking was generally the method of ensuring a place on board. The short stages had one major disadvantage. They were not allowed to pick up or set down passengers anywhere within the 'stones' other than at their advertised destination. A journey within the 'stones' could be made by 'Hackney' coach (an ancestor of today's taxi) but not by short stage. The 1831 Hackney Coach Act broke the monopoly enjoyed by the hackney coaches and paved the way for the omnibus in the centre of London. But that was still two years away. Before that came Shillibeer.

George Shillibeer

George Shillibeer, a 32-year old coachbuilder, had watched with interest the introduction of a network of 'omnibus' routes in Paris in 1828. The omnibus was a new idea in urban transport. No advance booking, and running on a fixed route with passengers being able to board and alight anywhere along it, the omnibus was the brainchild of Stanislas Baudry who had brought his idea to the French capital after it had been a success in Nantes 240 miles away. It was there that the term 'omnibus' is supposed to have originated, for M. Baudry's terminus in the town was by a shop owned by a M. Omnes whose slogan apparently was 'Omnes Omnibus'. By the summer of 1828 Baudry's omnibuses were carrying 300 Parisians a day.

Meanwhile Shillibeer had been seeking a licence to operate cabriolets (one or two seat open carriages) but in the omnibus he saw an opportunity. He applied to the Treasury for permission to begin a Paris-style omnibus service in London, but was refused because he would have encroached upon the hackney coach monopoly within the 'stones'. Shillibeer found a way round that one . . . literally. He planned his service to run from the Bank to Paddington by way of the New Road and The Angel, the equivalent of today's Marylebone, Euston and Pentonville Roads, which skirted the northern fringe of the 'stones'. He built two 20-seater coaches which bore the legend OMNIBUS on the side panels; Shillibeer had decided to stick with the French description, not such a bad thing when you consider that the suggested English names included 'Economist' and 'Folks-wain'. His 'Omnibus' service, initially with one coach but later with two, commenced on 4th July 1829 and ran to a strict three-hourly interval timetable, beginning at 9.00 am at Paddington and 10.00 am at Bank. A flat-fare of one shilling (5p) was charged for any distance travelled. The Omnibus proved so popular that within days Shillibeer's 'persons of great respectability' as his publicity described the conductors, were having to turn away customers.

Shillibeer's original green and yellow omnibuses were box-shaped saloons pulled by three horses harnessed side-by-side. There were three windows on each side interspersed by panels on which were painted the names of places passed en route and the destinations. Passengers entered and left the vehicle by a rear door. Inside a bench seat ran along the sides and front, allowing around twenty people to be accommodated, far more than the short stages and hackney coaches. The driver sat on a seat at the front above the horses, level with the roof, while the conductor stood on the rear step and collected the fares as passengers left the vehicle.

The Board of Stamps, which controlled the hackney coaches and the short stages, levied a tax on the operation of all passenger-carrying coach services, the amount depending on the number of horses between the shafts. Very soon Shillibeer reduced his horse-power to two, and built smaller 16-seat Omnibuses to compensate.

The buses which came onto the scene to compete with Shillibeer in the early 1830s were built to this same basic pattern. They were fairly primitive, having no heating or lighting. Straw was strewn on the floor to collect any muck brought in on muddy boots. The success of the omnibus was matched only by the over-zealous hustle for passengers by an increasing number of proprietors, many former short stage operators, whose colourful vehicles were rapidly establishing themselves on the streets of London.

It wasn't long before Shillibeer and his rival horse bus operators began co-operating to try to bring some order and sanity to the chaotic situation which prevailed along the New Road. By the early 1830s ninety omnibuses were plying for hire in the area and it was mutually agreed that the number be reduced to 57, operating at three-minute intervals. Control of the service would be the responsibility of inspectors at key locations along the route.

The setting up of this Association, the first of many similar bodies created down the years, and the measures it adopted to provide its customers with something akin to a regular service, was not only the first attempt to co-ordinate activity for mutual benefit, it was also Shillibeer's last contribution to London bus history. He had already been declared bankrupt and, following several abortive attempts to run profitable coach services elsewhere, plus a short spell in prison following a flight to France to escape his creditors, he became an undertaker. He died in 1866 but, even today, George Shillibeer is still spoken of as the man who first brought the idea of the bus to London.

The removal of the hackney coach monopoly in the 'stones' opened up unlimited opportunities for the expansion of the omnibus concept and came as significant improvements were being made to London's road network. New roads were built connecting areas which previously had no direct link between them, new bridges spanned the Thames at Vauxhall, Waterloo and Southwark, and many important and established thoroughfares were widened creating greater, and easier, mobility – ideal conditions for the omnibus to thrive.

Traditionally coach operators had written out tickets for their passengers but the short distances and constant coming and going of omnibus travel did not make practical such a laborious task. So London's first bus passengers just paid their fares to the conductor as they left the bus, not knowing whether their copper coins would ever reach the bus company coffers. It was generally recognised that conductors kept back some of the takings to share with drivers and horsekeepers.

By 1834 there were 620 horse buses licensed in London, and the number had doubled by 1850. By 1840 reductions in the level of taxes paid by the omnibus proprietors had enabled them to introduce cheaper fares. An Omnibus Guide published at the time of the Great Exhibition in 1851 listed over 150 different routes serving the capital and its environs. Service intervals varied from between five and twenty minutes for routes in inner London, to hourly or longer for those travelling to outlying districts on the fringes of what is now bustling Greater London. Many of the horse bus proprietors had formed themselves into Associations of the kind pioneered by Shillibeer, in an effort to reduce the competition for passengers which could, at times, become quite violent. A member proprietor was allotted certain 'times' when he could operate his vehicles on routes which were operated by his parent Association. It did not matter if these 'times' fell in slack periods because all the Association members received a share of the total receipts.

An early competitor of George Shillibeer's was Walter Hancock, who in 1833 began a steam bus service along the same route. He appears to have been the only person to use anything other than horses to move his buses this early. The vehicle illustrated dates from 1836.

The Birth of the Double-Decker

From the earliest days of buses some intrepid travellers climbed up onto the roof if no seats were available 'inside'. As buses grew in popularity more people braved the experience of riding on top, and many buses were fitted with a second seat behind the driver. Some of the newer buses had more sharply curved roofs which at busy times were used as perches by hardy male passengers sitting on the apex of the curve facing outwards. It was only a matter of time before someone built a bus with proper seating on the roof and in 1847 Adams & Company of Bow duly obliged with their Improved Omnibus. This had a longitudinal seat that was in fact the top of a clerestory roof which passengers would reach by stepping on metal rungs either side of the rear entrance. The new design had the additional advantage of increasing headroom in the main saloon. The rear platform was now illuminated at night, albeit fairly dimly, by oil lamps.

Thus was born the London double-deck bus. The new vehicles were put into service by the Economic Carriage Company, which charged half fare to those brave enough to ride on top.

There was an urgent need to increase capacity. The Great Exhibition held in Hyde Park in 1851 brought tens of thousands of visitors to London and a bonanza for the owners of the 1,300 or so horse buses then registered in the capital. Many proprietors hastily installed a longitudinal seat along the roofs of their vehicles. The seat became known as the 'knifeboard' because for some reason people associated it with the domestic felt-covered board used for

The 'outside' as the upper deck was called received proper seating in the late 1840s and Thomas Tilling's Knifeboard omnibus was typical of the breed which carried Londoners around the capital in the second half of the nineteenth century. Those 'outside' could tell the driver when they wished to alight, but those 'inside' usually captured his attention by banging sharply on the saloon roof. However in 1839 a London firm called Holtzapffel & Company developed a more refined method. This was a bell and cord arrangement, the bell being placed next to the driver and connected to the cord inside the bus. Curiously the invention was not an immediate success, the traditional bang on the roof approach taking many years to fade away. LT Museum

cleaning knives at home. Passengers sat along the seat facing outwards, and this rather precarious arrangemerit seemed to overcome the capacity problem with surprisingly few mishaps.

A sharp decline in business after the Great Exhibition closed brought forth little money, or incentive, for anyone to develop further the basic design of the omnibus, so for the next few years its shape remained unchanged. More stringent vehicle checks, administered by the police, were introduced in 1853, resulting in many buses being taken off the road. By 1854 only about 800 were licensed, and those which were running grew shabby.

A new era of road improvements began in London in 1855 with the creation of the Metropolitan Board of Works and London's first railways were opening, bringing more people into the capital. These happier conditions should have brought a change in the fortunes of the remaining omnibus proprietors but they didn't, at least not until inspiration came once again from Paris where the art of running buses was being perfected.

The creation by three French businessmen of the London General Omnibus Company in 1856 revitalised the industry. Starting in January of that year with 27 vehicles, by the end of 1856 the LGOC had 600 horse buses in its fleet, making it the largest bus company in the world. Within a few months of taking up the reigns the LGOC was holding a competition, with a £100 prize, to find a more suitable design of bus. The winner was Mr R. Miller of Hammersmith who saw many of his suggestions incorporated into a new vehicle. It was larger than previous models, six feet high instead of five with a width increase of six inches. It had a clerestory roof with a single longitudinal seat on top. Metal plates rather than rungs gave access to the upper deck.

The bus carried 26 passengers, 12 inside and 14 on top, a capacity which was to remain standard for the next 30 years. Inside, mats replaced the straw but in time the mats would be replaced by slatted wood floors. Delivery of the new buses was slow, and many of the existing ones were modified to give more headroom and safer access to the roof area. A number were fitted with a panel along each side of the upper deck. These panels became known as 'decency boards' and they acted as a safety barrier, the ideal advertisement board and as a screen to discreetly hide the ankles of the ladies who were now venturing up to the top deck.

In 1869 the mileage duty which had long been a burden to horse bus owners was abolished. Less burdened by tolls and taxes, benefiting from cheaper horse feed and with access to new and wider thoroughfares and bridges, the way was cleared for the further development of services and the debut of new bus companies. Of these the London Road Car, formed in 1881, is noteworthy because its new vehicles contributed to the evolution of the London bus. However its first attempt failed to capture any hearts. It was a new design of knifeboard bus with a front-mounted staircase and a front, instead of a rear, entrance. Passengers did not like this about-face approach, but undaunted the Road Car pressed on and later in 1881 unveiled what proved to be the last important development in horse bus design. This was the 'garden seat' omnibus, a design featuring wooden slatted upper deck seats facing the direction of travel. The top deck was now reached by a curved staircase leading from an enlarged left-hand rear platform, itself a new feature with its origins in

Regent Street in mid-Victorian times with two Knifeboard omnibuses gently making their way towards Oxford Circus. The conductors are in their designated place on the rear step. As can be seen, uniforms for conductors had yet to be introduced.

an Act of Parliament of 1867 which required all buses operating within four miles of Charing Cross to pick up and set down passengers on the left hand side of the road. Hitherto buses could pull into whichever kerbside a passenger desired, but as road traffic increased this practice became more dangerous. Eventually the requirement was extended throughout the Metropolis. Passengers liked the new buses, especially the garden seats, and many earlier buses were rebuilt to conform, although the process took time. The 'knifeboards' thus remained a familiar sight in London until the 1890s, except that by then many had acquired a new curved staircase.

The horse bus had reached its watershed. Internal illumination was improved in the 1890s with the introduction of acetylene lamps but weight was still the main factor restricting its further development. A vehicle of increased size and with a covered top deck, which was about the only new thing left to try, would have been considerably heavier, and therefore dependent on more horses to pull it. Horse feed fluctuated in price with the seasons, and any increase in its requirement without a proportional return in revenue was not even to be contemplated in an industry which was still at that time in private hands.

This view of a Tilling Garden Seat omnibus on its way to Putney shows clearly the new style seating arrangement 'outside', which a number of hardy souls have braved on a damp day, compared with the traditional longitudinal style seating still used in the saloon. Tilling obviously took advantage of the business opportunities available to him in south London, supplying carriages for weddings as well as horses for ordinary work.
LT Museum

Horse bus passengers soon associated the colour of the local omnibuses with the Associations which operated them and the routes they worked. In most cases details of the route were painted along the vehicle sides as the route was rarely altered. In later years horse buses were fitted with moveable destination boards which were usually positioned above or below the side windows.

In its final form the horse bus was a very different creature from Shillibeer's original of 70 years before, but a horse bus was still no match for a horse tram, which could carry large numbers of people at far less cost because of the lower horsepower required for a tracked vehicle. By 1900 tramway systems had been established in many parts of London and, as with the buses, there were a variety of different companies involved in their operation. Many of these had been in existence since the early 1870s and eventually most of those which operated in the County of London were acquired by the London County Council, which also proceeded to extend the system.

By 1898 discussions were under way on how best to electrify the tramways. It was obvious that electrification would enable cheap high-capacity transport to be provided by tramcars to the detriment of the buses. The Road Locomotive Act of 1865 had limited the speed of mechanically propelled trackless vehicles, such as they were, to a hair-raising two miles an hour in towns. To make matters worse all self-propelled vehicles had to be accompanied by someone carrying a red flag. In 1896 the speed limit was increased to a more acceptable 12mph, and the red flag consigned to the history books.

Buses are now in competition with trams, as this view in Upper Street, Islington shows, but the LGOC Garden Seat omnibus still has a healthy load, as do the following buses. The sender of the picture postcard from which this illustration is taken wrote approvingly of the horse buses and the time they gave to watch the passing view.

The Motor Age

Self-propelled buses were nothing new. Since the early years of the nineteenth century countless experiments had been carried out. As mentioned on page 6, Walter Hancock had in 1833 conducted trials with passenger-carrying single-deck steam carriages and achieved some success, but at the time no-one, except of course Hancock, felt confident enough to invest in the venture.

The repeal of the Locomotive Act brought down the barriers restricting horseless carriages and numerous experiments with steam as well as electric and petrol-engined buses were carried out, and several new companies were formed just to exploit them. Such was the flurry of activity surrounding horseless buses around the turn of the century that it is probably easiest to list the main developments as they affected London's buses chronologically:

1889 A Radcliffe-Ward single-deck battery-electric bus was tried out but does not appear to have run in passenger service.

1891 The Metropolitan Police licensed a battery operated double-deck bus seating 26 (12 inside and 14 upstairs) to run between Charing Cross and Victoria. It weighed 3¼ tons and, by all accounts, was slow.

1897 The London Electric Omnibus Company experimented with a ten-seater single-deck Radcliffe-Ward battery bus with more success than the previous attempts. Although the bus was never used in passenger service it made several demonstration trips and managed on one occasion to attain an average speed of 8mph! Also in 1897 the firm Pioneer ran a Lifu oil-fired steam bus for a short time.

1898 The London Steam Omnibus Company was formed by H.J. Lawson to operate a small fleet of French De Dion single-deck steam buses, but the plan did not materialise, so in 1899 the firm ordered forty Daimler petrol-engined single deckers and changed its name to the Motor Traction Company Ltd. It seems that only two such buses were ever operated, rather unsuccessfully.

1899 A 24-seat double-deck steam bus built by E. Gillett & Company of Hounslow was tried out by the Motor Omnibus Syndicate. The vehicle consisted of an adaptation of a horse bus body, mounted on a steam lorry chassis, and could accommodate 24 people. A large chimney protruded through an awning which covered the top deck.

1901 The South Western Motor Car Company operated a handful of ten-seat Daimler wagonettes in the Streatham and Balham areas, but their limited capacity meant that the revenue they earned was outweighed by the cost of running them, so they were soon withdrawn.

1902 The first London motor bus to have solid rubber tyres appeared in the autumn when the Motor Traction Company put a 12hp Daimler double decker into service. The same year London Road Car mounted a horse bus body on a steam powered chassis, but this strange machine was soon superseded by a Gillett double-deck steam bus.

1904 By this time two manufacturers, Daimler and Scott-Stirling, were in the forefront of motor bus development. London Road Car purchased two Daimlers, a move soon followed by many other busy horse bus operators.

The London Motor Omnibus Syndicate may well have the honour of running the first minibuses in the Capital, but it did not have a long life. These little vehicles ran for just three and a half months before the company went into liquidation in March 1903.

The London Road Car Company built up a sizeable fleet of motor buses before being amalgamated with the LGOC in 1908. This example is a Clarkson steam powered bus of 1905.

The Victoria Omnibus Company was one of many small independent horse bus operators to progress to motor buses, but in 1907 it went bankrupt. The bus illustrated is a 1906 Orion with horizontal engine.

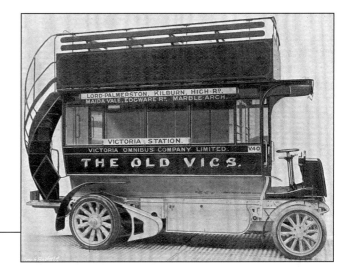

The General Takes the Plunge

Few of the many and varied vehicles which chugged onto the London bus scene in the first years of the twentieth century saw long service. It was easy of course for a small operator to buy one or two motor buses for prestige if nothing else, but the LGOC preferred a more cautious approach rather than risk buying a large quantity of untried vehicles with the possibility of disastrous results. It was the era of the Straker-Squire, the Orion, the Wolseley, De Dion, Darracq, and Büssing, so the General had no shortage of different chassis to choose from. In 1904 the company took the plunge and tested an American Fischer petrol-electric chassis mounted with a 30-seat double-deck body. The bus was not a success, but undaunted the LGOC set aside £20,000 for further motor bus experimentation. A number of different makes were tried, including a Clarkson single-deck steam bus, a German Orion with a horse bus body, a Leyland Crossley and a Milnes-Daimler. In all the General tested over thirty different chassis, available in an ever expanding market. Its first big orders for motor buses came in 1905 when it purchased 54 De Dion and 50 Büssing chassis. That year the company built its first motor bus garage at Dollis Hill.

In fact all efforts seem to have been geared towards experimenting with different traction methods rather than developing body designs, but some seemingly unimportant changes took place between 1905 and 1908 which nonetheless had quite far-reaching effects. For example in 1907 the London General Omnibus Company decided to paint its buses in a predominantly red livery, thus ending a tradition which had existed for most of the horse bus era where vehicles operating on particular routes were, regardless of proprietor, painted in the same basic colours.

In a similar way most operators replaced the location names painted on the sides of the buses with fleet names like VANGUARD (London Motor Omnibus Company), UNION JACK (London Road Car) and GENERAL (LGOC). In fact in 1905 the LGOC had produced a circle and bar symbol which it applied to its bus sides. This was developed in later years to become the symbol of the Underground Group, London Transport and, today, the operating arms of Transport for London.

Facing page The motor bus has arrived and is now dominant over the horse-bus, a solitary example of which can be seen on Royal Blue route 66 between two of the General's motor buses heading towards Marble Arch. The bus on route 15 is a De Dion dating from 1906. Beyond the junction of Oxford Street and Regent Street, behind Walters & George, can be seen the Oxford Circus station of the Baker Street & Waterloo Railway, opened in 1906. Adjacent to it is the Central London Railway's station of six years earlier. LT Museum

Below The length of a motor bus could be reduced by the use of a casing below the driver's seat for the engine. This Wolseley design is one of a number of types tested by the LGOC in 1904/5. It carries on its side the earliest form of the 'bullseye' (or 'roundel') logo still familiar today. This vehicle would have been among the first to carry it.

Below right The General had around 208 Milnes-Daimler motor-buses all built around 1905 as part of its enthusiastic conversion to mechanical propulsion. LT Museum

The arrival of the motor age brought mixed fortunes for the proprietors. There was more competition which, naturally, led to another round of amalgamations. In 1908 Vanguard and Union Jack merged with the General, which subsequently adopted Vanguard's unique route numbering system which had been instituted in 1906. For the first time many of London's principal routes were given numbers, some of which still relate to the same routes today, like the 9, 16 and 22.

Vanguard maintained a vehicle overhaul works in Walthamstow and had planned to build buses there. The newly-enlarged LGOC lost no time in taking over the plant and adopting it as its own vehicle chassis construction and development centre.

In 1909 the first new bus emerged from the Walthamstow plant. This was the X-type, a 28hp, 34-seat double decker. It was soon joined by 60 similar vehicles, many of which remained in service until May 1920.

For the next 50 or so years the development and style of the London bus lies

The 61-strong X-type built in 1909 have the distinction of being the first batch of buses built by the General at the Walthamstow factory it acquired from Vanguard and were thus the first motor buses purpose built for London conditions. The X-type was soon put in the shade by the B-type, launched the following year, but they soldiered on until 1920. Here X 54 rests in Middle Row garage after a stint on route 7.

almost exclusively in the hands of the LGOC and its successor, London Transport. True there were many independently-run bus companies right up until 1934, but the buses they used were types which were readily available from the manufacturers and found in towns and cities up and down the country. Many of these companies joined the LGOC pool along the way, after which established London types, in 'alien' liveries, could be found operating on their routes.

The motor age had truly arrived. For the General it was fully realised on 26th October 1911, for on the previous evening the last of the company's horse buses running on a route between Moorgate and London Bridge had been withdrawn. Almost three years later, on 4th August 1914, London's very last horse bus, operated by Thomas Tilling, ran between Honor Oak and Peckham Rye, ending an 85 year period of London's transport history and severing the last direct link between the short stages of Georgian London and the B-type, the first truly standard London motor bus.

In this view, typifying bus travel just prior to the Great War, a National Steam Car Clarkson stands with its crew prior to departing on the long journey from Peckham to Petersham. By 1914 National were the LGOC's biggest competitor on the streets of London.

B 420, seen here working on route 67 from Tottenham garage typifies the B in its post war form. The driver still has little protection against the elements, and the passengers little protection against the bumps caused by the solid tyres negotiating cobbled streets.

The B-type and Beyond

The General's X-type had been a reasonable success, apart from some design problems with the gearbox, and further development work was carried out at Walthamstow. The result emerged in October 1910 as the B-type. It weighed 3 tons 1¼ cwt (3622 kg), was 19ft 2ins long by 6ft 1¼ ins wide (5.85m x 2.10m) and 12ft 5ins (3.78m) high. Like the X-type it seated 34 passengers, 16 in the saloon and 18 'outside' as the upper deck was still known. The driver sat above and behind the 29.8hp four-cylinder engine. Although the Bs did not look very different from the other motor buses of the day they were undoubtedly the most reliable. Their careful design and manufacture allowed for interchangeability of parts, a quality which made for easier maintenance. By 1914 the General had 2,500 B-types in service, including some single deckers with 16-seater bodies. B-type chassis were being produced faster than the LGOC's North Road works could build the bodies, so a handful of other companies, like Hurst Nelson of Motherwell, provided B-type bodies as well. During the Great War some 1,300 B-types were sent to France as troop carriers, a valuable contribution to the war effort from which many returned to see out their days in London, days which ended for the double-deck version in 1926.

The first B-types were built under different circumstances to the later ones. In January 1912 the LGOC had become part of the Underground Group, and a consequence of this merger was the incorporation of the Walthamstow plant into a separate company within the Group. It was named the Associated Equipment Company, better known as AEC, three letters which were to become inseparable from the notion of reliability and quality in Britain's heavy commercial vehicle industry over the next 60 years.

Even Daimler, one of AEC's competitors, had a stake in the new company. In 1912 the Metropolitan Electric Tramways had decided to form a bus company to

In 1911, The Metropolitan Electric Tramways Company, wary about the threat of bus competition on its lucrative tramway routes in north and north west London, decided to form a bus company to fight the opposition. Eventually 225 buses, all Daimlers, were in the MET fleet, the company even building some of the bodies itself at its Hendon works. The bulk of the bodies were by Brush, ironically a major tramcar body builder at the time. The MET joined the LGOC in the Underground Group combine in 1912 after which its buses, like D 57 at Cricklewood, were on the same side so to speak.

complement its tramway network in north and north-west London. For this it had ordered 100 of the new Daimler CC chassis developed by Frank Searle, former Chief Motor Engineer of the LGOC and a leading figure in the design of the B-type. Under the merger, the LGOC took over the MET's bus operation and, therefore, its new Daimlers. The maintenance contract which MET had negotiated with Daimler was no longer required and as compensation to Daimler the LGOC appointed them as agents to sell any chassis built at AEC surplus to the General's own requirements. This arrangement also led to Daimler supplying engines for London buses and explains why some vehicles produced before 1930 are documented as having ADC (Associated Daimler) rather than AEC engines. All MET Daimlers were sent to France as troop carriers during the Great War and none returned to London service afterwards.

The AEC factory developed a new chassis – the Y-type – during the Great War and 12,000 were built for military vehicles. Few ever found their way under bus bodies, but the high quantity produced in a relatively short space of time illustrates the efficiency and high production capabilities attained by AEC which entered the 1920s with the ability and desire to produce bus chassis for an ever-increasing market at home and overseas.

The first significant break from conventional bus body design since the garden-seat horse bus came in the summer of 1919 when the LGOC unveiled its new K-type. The K had a larger body than the B-type, at 22ft 7ins long (6.90m) by 7ft 1in (2.16m), and its construction incorporated rear wheel arches so that the saloon sat over the rear wheels rather than between them. This enabled some transverse seating to be fitted in the lower-deck, replacing the longitudinal side benches, a feature of bus design since Shillibeer. The K seated 46 passengers, 22 inside and 24 out. Later about 100 Ks had longitudinal seating fitted inside which reduced the total seating capacity to 44.

Another new feature introduced with the K-type was that the driver's position was now beside, rather than behind, the engine, a system known as forward control. The K-type thus pioneered the half-cab layout which remained a feature on buses in London and throughout the country until the 1960s. The 28hp Ks were easier to steer and, like their forebears, had solid rubber tyres, a fact of little importance since they were legally restricted to only 12mph. The Ks also had a bell and cord arrangement for signalling the driver. In all 1,132 K-types were built for or acquired by the LGOC between 1919 and 1928. The class included 24 single deckers, built in 1925, noteworthy in that they were the first General buses with pneumatic tyres.

Of all the bus types built by the General during the 1920s the Ks, which were the smallest, proved most useful little vehicles when the company came to extend its services into the newly developing suburbs and country towns around London. Most K-type bodies were built by the General but some were supplied by Brush, Strachans and Shorts. Quite large numbers of double-deck vehicles were later given single-deck bodies. Withdrawal of the Ks began when the fourth generation of General motor buses began to arrive in quantity in 1930, the last K running in passenger service on 22nd June 1932.

The Ks were able to provide more seats for the ever-increasing volume of London bus passengers – the General carried 936 million in 1920 – but the company knew it could build a bus to carry even more. It pressed the authorities for permission to build a larger and therefore heavier bus, and in December 1920 produced the first S-type, which although in the same style as the K had a longer (24ft 8ins) body. The S could accommodate 54 passengers, 26 in the saloon and 28 on top. The 35hp engine had no difficulty in pulling the 4tons 10cwt unladen weight of the S, and the police soon increased the laden weight limitation from 7 to 8½ tons, allowing more of the type to be built. The total eventually reached 928 including 79 single deckers later fitted or built with pneumatic tyres. Many of these were operated by National and East Surrey and some of them lasted into London Transport days, but all the double deckers had gone by December 1931.

London's first half-cab design (the K-type) is seen behind its higher capacity successor, the S-type, in Wimbledon. The K is on a special service between Wimbledon station and the tennis ground.
David Ruddom collection

The chocolate liveried 'Express' buses of A.G. Partridge began a phase of often heated competition on central London bus routes in the 1920s.
Glyn Kraemer-Johnson

Competition and Progress

After the First World War the gradual progress towards unification of all London's transport continued, spearheaded by Albert Stanley, who became Lord Ashfield in 1920, and Frank Pick. They failed to establish a working relationship with the municipal tramway operators, including the giant LCC undertaking, but they rode out a storm of renewed competition from independent operators in the early 1920s. This was a time when men returning from service in the Great War were anxious to get involved in any profitable enterprise, and running buses fitted the bill for many. First in line of the new wave of independents was Mr A.G. Partridge who began running his 'Express' bus alongside the General's on route 11 on 5th August 1922. His open-top chocolate and cream painted Leyland bus, which was soon joined by others, was immaculately turned out and, after the General stopped trying to impede its progress, ran efficiently. The good service that Express and some of the other independents provided gave them no small measure of respectability, some of which turned out to be misplaced as not all of the new breed of operators put public service first.

The swansong of the independents, which numbered over 250 during the period 1922–23, came in July 1927 with the formation of the London Public Omnibus Company which had 76 members/operators. The following year the LGOC reached a co-ordinated services and fares agreement with the Public, and took it over completely in 1929, effectively bringing to an end a colourful, if not a little hectic, era in London's bus history.

Most of London's buses had been double-deck since 1850, but in wet and cold weather the capital had a fleet of buses which were really nothing more than single deckers; for who but the hardy, or foolhardy, would want to travel 'outside' in driving rain or arctic temperatures? True, the bus companies fitted tarpaulins to the backs of the upper deck seats to help keep people dry should it rain, but in such conditions a bus was no match for a tramcar, most of which by 1920 were fully enclosed, or at least had covered top decks.

The Metropolitan Police were wary about sanctioning covered tops on motor buses, believing that the additional height and weight would make the vehicles top heavy. They may have been right, and the LGOC did not try to prove otherwise by even attempting to fit a covered top to a K or S. But in 1922 the General and AEC produced a bus with a much lower chassis frame than any previously built. The lower deck was reached by just one 13-inch step up from the ground instead of the usual two. The General christened the new bus NS, believed by some to stand for the Latin 'nulli secundus' – second to none. It seated 50 passengers (24 downstairs and 26 up). The new design of chassis frame made the bus eminently suitable for fitting with a covered top, and NS 1 duly appeared with one as part of its integral design. Although double deckers with roofs were by that time running successfully in cities like Birmingham and Liverpool, the ever-cautious Metropolitan Police refused to allow NS 1 to enter service in this form. The NS was thus launched on London's travelling public with little in its favour besides a lower entrance step.

The first NSs entered service on route 11 in May 1923, and over a thousand had been built by the time the police relented and permitted London's buses to have covered top decks. From 1925, the remaining NS buses were built with covered tops, and eventually most of the 1,700 open-toppers of the class received them as well. The first London buses with covered tops ran in October 1925 from Loughton Garage on route 100 (Elephant & Castle – Epping).

In its new form the NS weighed in at 6tons 6cwt and proved to be a very reliable vehicle. Twenty-five NSs built for the Blackwall Tunnel service went

Specially posed with driver and conductor suitably kitted out in summer garb, LT Museum exhibit NS 1995 is the sole survivor of the mainstay class in London's bus fleet in the mid to late twenties. Originally an open-topper with solid tyres and an open cab, it later received a covered top and pneumatic tyres to bring it into line with newer buses.
LT Museum

one step forward and one back. They had fully enclosed staircases to the top deck which, because the sides were more tapered to allow for tunnel wall clearance, had knifeboard-style longitudinal seating running its full length.

By the time the NS was in production at AEC the company, which had begun life as an exclusively London bus builder, was selling chassis at home and overseas and of course the General's associates, East Surrey and National amongst them. NSs were thus as familiar a sight in Buenos Aires as they were in Battersea or Box Hill. The last of the class, built in 1928, had wind-down windows which were to be a feature on London's buses for the next 40 years.

In 1927 the LGOC took delivery of 12 large-capacity 6-wheelers which were grouped into one class and coded LS (London Six). One was a 34-seat single decker, but the rest were double deckers originally seating between 64 and 70. All were fitted with pneumatic tyres, becoming the first General double deckers to have them; eventually most of the NSs received them as well. Pneumatic tyres enabled the General's buses to give passengers faster and more comfortable rides, although initially the buses fitted with them were confined to suburban services.

The giant LSs, up to that time the largest London buses built, originally had ADC engines. They appeared as AEC's association with Daimler came to an end and as AEC transferred its chassis production to a new factory in Southall to the west of London. The new works was some 16 miles from Walthamstow and some transportation of staff between the two locations was necessary. AEC built a special 104-seater 6-wheel bus to ferry staff between the two places.

Although the 12 LSs were by no means uniform in appearance or specification, LS 9 illustrated here is representative of the bulk of the class, open-staircased and seating 70. By all accounts these huge buses were slow, even by the standards of the day which restricted bus speeds to 12mph.
Glyn Kraemer-Johnson

The Three Rs — Renown, Reliance and Regent

In 1929 there were celebrations. The bus was a hundred years old. A full-size representation of Shillibeer's Omnibus was built and paraded with buses old and new. These included LT 1, a brand new bus with a modern 54-seat Chiswick-built body sitting snugly on a new AEC Renown chassis with its 120 bhp 6-cylinder petrol engine. It was the most up-to-date bus in the General's fleet and compared favourably with the new Leyland Titan double deckers which were in the hands of some of the General's independent adversaries. The Titan, and its single-deck counterpart, the Tiger, had been designed by G.A. Rackham, Leyland's Chief Engineer, and produced in 1927 and 1929 respectively. The new buses were quite revolutionary, having a 6-cylinder engine, 4-speed gearbox, and unique chassis frame which permitted a body with a lower gangway to be fitted.

Daimler's split with AEC in 1928 coincided with the departure of Associated Equipment's Chief Engineer, Charles Edwards. Who better to fill the vacancy at Southall than Rackham, who accepted AEC's offer and lost no time in producing a new chassis – the Reliance. It was followed in 1929 by three very advanced petrol engine chassis christened Regal, Regent and Renown – names which were to be linked with Britain's buses for the next three decades. The Regal was a chassis primarily for single deckers, the Regent for double deckers, whilst the Renown was a 6-wheel chassis capable of taking either type of body. By the end of 1929 the General had launched three new classes each based on the new chassis. The new buses had advanced body styling which gave them a sturdier and more substantial appearance than the NS, K, or anything before.

LT 1 entered service on route 16A (Victoria – Cricklewood) on 6th August 1929. It was clad in a striking new livery; the lower panels were in the familiar red, but the rest of the bus was painted cream and lined out in black. The headlights were mounted next to the new-style radiator, one of the first to sport the famous AEC blue triangle badge. All very modern for its time, until you came to look at the back – for there, looking very odd on such a modern bus, was a traditional open staircase, a feature which also adorned the next 149 LTs built in the early months of 1930. These subsequent buses were in a more conventional livery of red with pearl grey window surrounds, silver roof and black mudguards. The first 50 LTs, and ST 1, the first of the new Regents, had glazed driver's cabs, but the Public Carriage Office ruled such an innovation dangerous on double deckers. Subsequent deliveries of both types returned to the open-cab format, the cab being designed so that windows could be fitted later should the PCO change its attitude, which it did later in 1930.

The Regent chassis STs closely resembled the LTs but at 25 feet in length were 1ft 9ins shorter. Both types were 7ft 6ins wide, making them the widest General buses built so far. The STs, with their 98 bhp six-cylinder petrol engines, had seats for 49 passengers. The first people to ride in ST 1, which appeared in the same livery as the first LT and was first licensed in October 1929, were no doubt impressed by the fully enclosed staircase. The Regents found work with the LGOC's subsidiaries, East Surrey and Overground amongst them. Tillings had almost 200 open-staircase Regents, and these, together with other independently-owned Regents, passed to London Transport ownership in 1933 and were numbered in the ST series.

Facing page bottom This rare colour photo taken when ST 127 was new in May 1930 shows to full advantage some livery features that are sometimes difficult to distinguish in monochrome pictures. The dark red and chrome wheel hubs, black lining, white roof, and polished steel raised fleet number all combine with the gloss of the red and 'broken white' to give us a taste of what these handsome vehicles were like in their prime. Note also the absence of a glazed cab windscreen; these were not fitted until 1931 following objections by the police to the original design. When ST 127 ended its days at Upton Park garage in June 1949 its appearance no doubt reflected the many years of hard service it had put in both in peacetime and in wartime London.
LT Museum

Right Representing the LT class is LT 659 at Chingford, Royal Forest Hotel. The first LTs carried a much reduced destination display similar to that shown on ST 127 below, but later more generous information was provided as shown here.

The graceful lines of the single-deck LT are represented here by LT 1019, with its 35-seat Chiswick-built body sitting comfortably on its AEC Renown chassis. The bus, new in April 1931, passed to London Transport in 1933 and survived in service until January 1953, the final month the single-deck members of this famous class operated. It is seen early in its life working from Holloway garage, its first base. J. Higham

Both the initial batches of LTs and STs were fitted with roller blind indicator boxes replacing the detachable route boards used since early motor bus days. The blind apertures on the double-deckers were small, and only permitted the route number and destination to be displayed. Later deliveries had larger destination boxes incorporating roller blinds and these were fitted either to the panel below the top deck front windows or on the canopy over the driver's cab.

The fully enclosed London bus had arrived. The front canopy was now the only feature by which it could be traced back to the earliest motor buses of 30 years before, and the canopy disappeared from the last deliveries of LTs and STs in 1932. These had flush fronted bodies, and became known as the 'Bluebirds' because another 'first' they boasted was a blue-patterned seat moquette fitted over foam cushions. At last the London bus had said farewell to three of its traditional design traits, the open staircase, route boards and the front canopy.

In all there were 1,428 LTs, including two-hundred 35-seater single deckers. Seating capacity on later LT batches varied from 56 to 60. The number of STs eventually totalled 1,139. Although the General built most of the bodies for the LTs and STs, some bodywork for the latter was supplied by Strachans and Shorts.

In 1929 experiments had been proceeding with diesel engines. Three STs were fitted with oil engines (as they were then called) in December 1930 with a small batch of LTs receiving them the following year. Oil engines were to prove easier to maintain and longer lasting.

Above Fresh from the Metro-Cammell factory are these Dennis Lances, four out of a small fleet of 25 the LGOC bought for its Overground subsidiary in 1931/32. Numbered D 1–25 by Overground, they passed to London Transport in 1933 and became DL 1–25. Being non-standard they were sold in 1937.

Left The Bluebird was the last development of the LT design and with its flush front-end was the one which pointed the way to the future. LT 741 was the usual 6-wheel combination of Chiswick body and AEC Renown chassis. The generous blind display was surely much missed when wartime economies restricted route information to about three-quarters of the centre destination box.
Glyn Kraemer-Johnson

Nicely preserved T 31 is posed in idyllic surroundings to illustrate how the first batch of this famous class looked when brand new. The bus was built by the LGOC in December 1930 and was allocated to Nunhead garage for use on route 621, so the re-creation is pretty authentic. *Peter Plummer*

The first General buses to be based on AEC's new Regal chassis with its 95 bhp petrol engine were 50 single deckers built at Chiswick works in 1929. They were coded 'T' and the class has the distinction of being in production over the longest period, for the last one was delivered in 1948. The first Ts, which entered service in December 1929 (T 1 running from Hornchurch garage), had open rear platforms and seated 30 passengers. One of the first batch (T 38) was fitted with a 28-seat coach style body and set the style for the buses which were to be closely associated with the Green Line coach network for almost a quarter of a century. By 1938 the T class numbered over 700 vehicles, almost all of them with forward-entrance bodies purpose-built for Green Line. The Ts were a very stylish and hard-working class, lasting well into the post-war period.

T 211c a Duple-bodied AEC Regal, originally entered service from Romford garage on LGOC Green Line route from Charing Cross to Brentwood in January 1931. When this pre-war colour shot was taken it was still on Green Line service although working from the Board's remote Tunbridge Wells garage. It came from a 100-strong batch of Green Line T's which collectively had a chequered career few surviving into the post-war era. T 211 was one of sixteen commandeered by the War Department in May 1945 and shipped off to Germany.

Two 1936 posters publicising
Green Line express services.
LT Museum

Variety was added to the Green
Line fleet in the 1930s by
vehicles acquired from
operators of express coach
services within the London
Transport area. This 1930 built
Leyland with Duple body was
acquired from Premier Line and
lasted on Green Line work until
1938. J. Higham

The revolutionary Q-type of 1932 was a landmark in bus design and technological development. Its centre entrance full fronted body allowed seating to be placed alongside the driver's position. It entered service at Hammersmith garage on the 11 group of routes in September 1932. The choice of these busy double-deck routes for the debut of this unique bus was perhaps due to their passing close to the General's HQ at 55 Broadway, Westminster. It wasn't long before it found a new home at Nunhead garage on single-deck route 621. It ended its days as a country bus at Reigate garage, being disposed of in January 1946.
Glyn Kraemer-Johnson

Right Inside Q 1 offered comfort and style and a glimpse of the evolving design development of the London bus with smooth lines and good lighting. The fare from Shepherd's Bush to Liverpool Street was a mere 8d (3p), a far cry from the £1 of today.
LT Museum

Where's the Engine?

The single decker which stole the honours in the early 1930s, and which provided the bang with which the General ended its 77-year existence, was Q 1. It seems that the bus was given the Q code to denote secrecy during its development, as this was the classification which the Royal Navy gave to its secret craft during the First World War. Q 1, with its 27ft 5ins long chassis, broke away from convention by having its power unit, a 123 hp 6-cylinder petrol engine, positioned behind the offside front wheel beneath a longitudinal seat. This arrangement enabled more passengers to be carried. In fact the centre-door, full-fronted body could seat 37, two more than the single-deck LTs which were 20ins longer. Q 1 entered service on route 11E (Liverpool Street – Shepherds Bush) on 5th September 1932. It was joined in 1934 by four other prototypes, all double deckers based on the same side-engine principle. When new, Q 2 and Q 3 had 56-seater front-entrance Metro-Cammell bodies, with Q 4 and Q 5 being fitted with Weymann centre entrance bodies.

Q 2 along with Q 3 were built by the LPTB at Chiswick Works in 1934. Like Q 1 they were 4-wheelers. The entrance was at the front of the vehicle and the staircase was right behind the driver. In common with many of the official illustrations of buses at Chiswick Works the route information shown in the photograph on which this painting was based bore no relation to the route the bus ended up working. Both Q 2 and Q 3 went off to Harrow Weald to work on route 114. Like Q 1, Qs 2 and 3 ended up as country buses, this time at Grays garage in 1939. Both were stored during the war, Q 3 being scrapped in 1941 after suffering enemy damage. Q 2 was disposed of in March 1946. *Glyn Kraemer-Johnson*

Eventually the Q class numbered 238 vehicles, almost all of them single deckers, built to run on London Transport's central red bus, green country bus and Green Line services. Seating capacity varied between 32 and 37 depending on the tasks the buses were expected to perform, and the body building was shared between Park Royal Vehicles and the Birmingham Railway Carriage and Wagon Company. The production batches were fitted with 7.7 litre oil engines.

The later Qs, like Park Royal bodied Q 145 seen working from Cricklewood garage on route 226, retained the front entrance layout of Q 2 and Q 3, but overall design was more in keeping with mid-1930s single-deck styling. Q 145 entered service in April 1936 at Chalk Farm garage and was finally withdrawn in March 1953, being subsequently exported to Rangoon in 1955. This photograph shows it in 1948. Capital Transport

The interior of Southall garage early in London Transport years. The LPTB's own design of double-decker, the STL, rubs shoulders with acquired double-deckers. LT Museum

London Transport

In his 20 years in the service of the Underground Group and its predecessors, Lord Ashfield had constantly reaffirmed his commitment to a properly planned and co-ordinated transport system for London. The goal: cheap transport with the profits which came from the busiest services subsidising those which were just as socially necessary but which did not pay their way. Competition between transport modes and operators with conflicting fares made this worthy aim very difficult to achieve, but by the end of the 1920s much of the competition which predominantly affected the buses had, as we have seen, been removed. This prompted the promotion in Parliament of two transport co-ordination Bills, one by the Underground Group and the other by the London County Council, with the ultimate aim of creating a single management for their undertakings. By 1929 the Bills were almost through parliament when a snap General Election was held and a Labour administration was voted into office.

The Minister of Transport in the new Government was Herbert Morrison, a man with firm ideas on how London's transport should be developed; he did not allow the two co-ordination Bills to continue as they stood. In fact he devised a whole new structure for London's public transport with a governing Board to manage, plan and operate everything within a 25-mile radius from Charing Cross, except the main line railways which were to retain their autonomy but join the London traffic pool. The Board would be under public control, but non-political in its composition. It would have to be self-supporting because it would not be subsidised. The Labour government lasted only two years, being replaced in 1931 by a National Coalition government which appointed the Liberal Percy Pybus as its Minister of Transport. He supported Morrison's London Passenger Transport Bill and, after a somewhat protracted and sometimes difficult passage, the Bill received Royal Assent in April 1933. It came into effect on 1st July 1933, when the London Passenger Transport Board, or 'London Transport' as it was soon popularly known, assumed responsibility for all the services of the Underground Group, including the LGOC and its Country Services, as well as those of the Metropolitan Railway, all London's tramway undertakings, and the remaining independent bus companies in the Board's area, almost all of which had passed into London Transport control by the middle of 1934.

Chairman of the new Board was Lord Ashfield, with Frank Pick as his deputy. Unification of London's transport services had finally arrived, one hundred and two years after Shillibeer had chaired the first meeting of omnibus proprietors concerned at the effect unrestricted competition was having on their business. At the end of 1934 there were 5,976 buses and coaches in the Board's ownership. During the year they had carried some 1,950 million people over the 2,396 bus and coach route miles within the Board's 1,986 square mile territory, clocking up a grand total of 258,199,086 miles between them. The Board inherited 1,000 buses from the independents. Most of these joined the London Transport fleet, some surviving until early post-war days.

The remainder of the 1930s were years of remarkable achievement for the Board. One of the most notable achievements was the speed with which it managed to establish its identity. It was given a head start in that the best features of the Underground Group were carried over into the new organisation; fine architecture for Underground stations and other premises including bus garages, the 'bullseye' bar and circle symbol first used by the General in 1905 and Edward Johnston's clear sans serif typeface for signing and publicity, originally commissioned by Frank Pick for the Group in 1916. London Transport was soon producing comprehensive and colourful publicity with more than sufficient information about services contained in maps, leaflets and timetable books.

ABCDEFGHIJKL
MNOPQRSTUV
WXYZ abcdefgh
ijklmnopqrstuvw
xyz (&£.,:;'!?-*"")
1234567890

Longer 4-wheelers

In October 1932 Thomas Tilling had the distinction of receiving the first AEC STL-type chassis. Soon after, the company fitted this handsome 56-seat body to it and numbered it ST 837. It was to be the first of 80 buses operated by Tilling on behalf of the LGOC. Before they entered service the batch was renumbered STL 50–130, YY5351 becoming STL 51. In 1933 the whole batch was absorbed into the LPTB fleet, STL 51 surviving until April 1948.

In 1932 new legislation permitted the manufacture of a 4-wheel chassis with a greater distance between front and rear axles. The length was increased from 15ft 6ins, the wheelbase of the ST type, to 16ft 3ins. The main advantage of this change was a reduction in operating costs, since the cheaper 4-wheel layout could carry just as many passengers as a 6-wheeler.

AEC soon adapted their Regent chassis to accord with the new dimensions, but the first examples to see service in London were not with the LGOC but on buses built for an independent, Charles Pickup, who took delivery of five open-toppers with enclosed staircases early in 1932. The LGOC ordered 102 new-length chassis for its associate Thomas Tilling who built the bodies for them.

The advantages of the new longer chassis were outweighed by its unsuitability to take the 8.8-litre oil engine without exceeding the new length parameters. The oil engine was already proving its worth, giving more miles per gallon and using cheaper fuel. The new buses had to have reconditioned petrol engines displaced from LTs – but work was soon well in hand on the development of a lighter – 7.7-litre – oil engine.

The LGOC did not receive its first new Regent chassis until October 1932. A 60-seat body was built for it at Chiswick, and it was unveiled as STL1 to the press in December. The new bus resembled the flush-fronted 'Bluebird' design of the later LTs and STs; in fact the upper deck actually overhung the driver's cab by a few inches making the bus look slightly top heavy. The first STLs entered service on routes 8 and 60 from Clay Hall garage on 3rd January 1933. By July, when the General was absorbed into the LPTB, the number of STLs in service had reached 180 (although the total included those built by Tillings which were numbered in the same series).

The arrival of the STLs enabled many of the older buses inherited from the independents, as well as the NSs, to be withdrawn. The last NS ran on the evening of November 30th 1937. This example is a special variant built for the Blackwall and Rotherhithe tunnels.
LT Museum

The LGOC had long searched for the optimum capacity bus and had concluded that a large-capacity vehicle seating 60 or more, while seemingly the best option for busy routes, created fare collection problems for conductors. It was decided that a 56-seat bus was the best choice and in August 1933 STL 203 appeared with a new style Chiswick-built 56-seat body. It had a more tapered, leaning-back look, setting the style of the London double decker for the next 20 years.

STL 203 still bore the legend GENERAL on its side panels despite being among the first buses built for the LPTB; the fleet name LONDON TRANSPORT did not appear on buses until the spring of 1934. In all, 2,700 STLs were built in batches over 12 years, although the bulk of the class was in service by the outbreak of war in 1939. Each batch was different in some degree from the others and the class proved to be quite a mixed bag. The first STLs had a new-style three-in-one panel route destination layout which was to be a design feature on most London double deckers until 1978. The positioning of the boxes was altered on later deliveries and the last batches had the front route number contained in a roof-box similar to the later LT/ST vehicles. The STLs were used throughout the London Transport area. A small batch was built to low bridge dimensions by Metro-Cammell for services from the former East Surrey garage at Godstone. These vehicles are noteworthy in London bus development because they were the first to have driver's cab doors, a feature which never graced other members of the STL class. In addition there was a batch of country buses with front entrances, a small batch of 40 with humped roofs for the Blackwall and Rotherhithe tunnel routes, and a small quantity of low bridge buses for central and country bus work. Most STLs had Chiswick-built bodies, but some were constructed by Park Royal and Weymann, names which were to feature prominently in the post-war era of London's buses. In fact the last STLs were built by Weymann who turned out a small batch in 1945 with provincial style bodywork.

Standard Chiswick-bodied STL 607 negotiates Marble Arch on route 137, which in the mid-1930s was operated by Catford garage and ran from Highgate to Elmers End. LT Museum

Right GY 839 was originally one of four AEC Regent open-toppers built in 1932 for the independent Charles Pickup of Dulwich. It was absorbed into the LPTB fleet in 1933 and re-numbered STL 557. Soon after it received a covered STL-style top-deck, giving it the appearance, to the untrained eye at least, of a standard STL.

Below The Godstone STLs were a batch of 12 forward-entrance buses ordered by London General Country Services but not delivered until 1934, after the formation of the LPTB. For many years their home was on route 410 and these distinctive Weymann-bodied buses were a familiar sight on the borders of Kent and Surrey. They were destined for a long life with London Transport, the last being withdrawn in July 1953.
LT Museum

The ultimate development in STL bodywork design arrived in 1937. STL 2386 is seen in its pre-war condition. The silver roof was one of the first casualties of wartime when roofs were repainted brown to render them less visible from the air.

During the 1930s, London Transport had a contract with AEC for the supply of 90 per cent of its chassis. Most of the remainder were built by Leyland which received two valuable orders from the Board. The first was for two batches of Cub single deckers (C class). The Cubs were intended as replacements for the driver-only operated Dennis Darts and other small buses in the outer Central and Country areas. They were normal-control buses, unlike a further eight Cubs built in 1936 which were front-entrance forward-control vehicles with one and a half decks. These unique buses were built primarily for the Inter-Station night bus service, which linked several main line railway termini and which has survived in one form or other ever since. The other Leyland order was for 100 double-deck Titan chassis with standard Leyland bodywork tailored slightly to STL style. The buses, coded STD, proved extremely robust in London service, lasting just as long as the STLs, and were a familiar sight on the routes from Hendon garage, where they spent most of their lives.

Leyland Cubs were bought for quieter single-deck services in 1935 and 1936, seventy-five with Short bodies followed by twenty-two bodied by Weymann. LT Museum

1937 saw the entry into service of 100 Leyland Titans. London Transport's close association with AEC meant that Leyland was very much a minority supplier, though this was to change after the war when substantial orders for Leyland chassis were placed.
Glyn Kraemer-Johnson

One of the unique double-deckers of the 1930s was LT 1137. Built as an experimental double-deck Green Line coach in 1931, it was not considered successful in this role and was converted to country bus use in 1935.

The Bus Stop

Although buses ran on fixed routes, before the 1930s passengers could hail a bus wherever it suited them, and buses could stop anywhere, within reason, to pick up passengers or set them down. Convenient, but it could play havoc with bus running times, and as London's traffic increased so the problem became worse. In 1913 the LGOC experimented with a few fixed stops, but it wasn't until the 1920s that the Company introduced bus stops at the busiest places and actively encouraged passengers to use them. Even so, buses still had to stop when required, official stop or not.

The new London Passenger Transport Board soon grasped the nettle and began to increase the number of fixed stops, recognising that the stop-anywhere principle was contributing to service delays. It urged its customers to use the stops and in March 1935 introduced an experimental scheme whereby stops were placed along an entire stretch of route from Euston Road to Tottenham. The stops were either compulsory, where buses had to stop, or request, where passengers could either hail the bus they wanted to board or ring the bell once if they wished to alight. By 1937 nearly 150 miles of road had fixed stops and LT continued the strategy, either by fitting stops along specified routes or in designated areas. By the early post-war period the whole of LT's vast area had fixed bus stops.

The finishing touches are being put to some new bus stops at Chiswick Works in January 1936 in readiness for the introduction of fixed stopping places. Hulton

Bus Shelters

Shelters for bus passengers were few and far between in the early days, indeed most of the shelters in London were provided by the LCC Tramways Department for its more fortunate customers.

The LPTB wasted little time in designing and installing modern shelters with seating and good provision for route maps and publicity. In fact the first shelters erected in 1934/5 acted as a focal point for passengers to wait for buses, even before fixed stops were installed. They were stylish flat-roofed metal and glass affairs, and some of the early ones boasted one, or even two, large LT bullseyes on their roofs. During the war something a little less lavish was produced; this was the aluminium framed 'Q' shelter, which was little more than a free-standing frame bolted to the pavement. The 'Q' shelter, much beloved by children who happily spent the moments before their bus arrived by somersaulting over the cross bars was, in a modified form, produced until the 1960s. By this time some areas, especially the more exposed places, had been graced with handsome enclosed wooden structures like the 'Keston' designed by London Transport and named after the location of the first one to be installed. LT also purchased the wooden Astolet shelter recognisable by its pointed roof. Both types, unlike the very basic and exposed aluminium framed shelter, had seating.

This splendid, well proportioned, steel panelled shelter has ample space for timetable and London Transport's promotional publicity. The photograph is in Longbridge Road, Barking, opposite the bus garage.
LT Museum

The Era of Streamlining

The 1930s were perhaps the most inventive period of all in the history of the London bus; before the decade was over two further engine positions had been tried out on single deckers. In 1937 Leyland and the LPTB co-operated on the design of what was hitherto the most advanced chassis concept yet, an 8.6-litre oil engine turned 45 degrees and mounted under the floor within the chassis frame behind the driver's cab. Its single-deck Park Royal body resembled the then current design of T class Green Line coaches, except that the bonnet sloped sharply; the radiator was positioned at the bottom of the slope. The bus, TF 1, was the first of 88 single-deckers which included 13 Park Royal 33-seater private hire coaches. The remainder consisted of 34-seat Green Line coaches, built at Chiswick. When the post-war generation of single deckers arrived in the early 1950s some TFs were transferred to country bus work. The TFs, and the Cs, remained in regular service until 1953.

So where else could the engine go? Not in many other places surely, except perhaps at the back, and that is just where it was fitted in the CR type built jointly by Leyland and London Transport in 1939. These little 20-seaters had the same style bodies as the TFs, except that the 4.37-litre Cub engine and gearbox were placed at the rear of the vehicle. The 49 CRs were destined for a short life with London Transport. Being entirely different mechanically from other buses, the spare parts for them were in short supply, especially during the war, which broke out as the class was being built. The CRs were stored until 1946 when they reappeared to run mainly as peak-hour reliefs on busy services. The last ones were withdrawn in November 1953.

The legacy of this pre-war collaboration between Leyland and London Transport was the further experimentation which was carried out with rear-engine buses in the post-war years, resulting in the vehicle which was to turn the bus world about face in the late-1950s – the rear-engined Leyland Atlantean. But that was way in the future.

Facing page upper Full-fronted STL 857 was the LPTB's attempt to introduce modern streamlining into the STL design. The bus appeared late in 1935 and within a few weeks was re-classified STF 1. It was not, however, destined to be the first of an interesting STL sub-group. Drivers found the cab layout restrictive and noisy, so in May 1938 STF 1 became STL 857 once again, rebuilt with a standard half-cab layout and radiator grille. However, it was still recognisable because of its more raked back upper-deck front section, which no doubt inspired the designers of the RT later in the 1930s. LT Museum

Facing page lower The TF, with its horizontally mounted underfloor engine, represented another significant advance in bus design. The 88 strong class included twelve Private Hire coaches (TF 2–13) with 33-seat Park Royal bodies sporting glass panelled roofs. On 23rd October 1940 LT's non-operational bus park at Bull Yard, Peckham was bombed and many buses, along with eleven of the twelve Private Hire TFs, including TF 9 seen here, were destroyed. LT Museum

Right A CR operates a 'relief' journey on route 73 in post-war London. Although the 49 CRs had a patchy and short-lived existence with London Transport their part in the development of the motor-bus during the twentieth century was an important one. Two of them, CR 16 and CR 36, are in preservation.

Wartime

Above A first casualty of war. ST 373 was involved in a disastrous collision with a car on the first night of 'blackout' restrictions, 1st September 1939, in Staines Road, Twickenham.

Above right Many main roads out of London, such as the A41, became one-way streets to speed the evacuation of school-children over the weekend of 1st–3rd September 1939 when war had become inevitable.

During the years 1934 to 1939 the bus fleet grew from 5,976 to 6,389. We can only imagine how this trend would have continued had the Second World War not intervened. The war was to have a serious effect on London Transport, and especially its bus services, with 166 buses being lost, more vehicles than some provincial operators had in their entire fleets, and with countless others being damaged. B-type buses had been put into military transport use in the First World War, and in 1939 it was the 9T9 and 10T10 Green Line coaches that were called up. Green Line services were suspended and the vehicles converted for use as ambulances.

Just before the war AEC had developed a new chassis powered by a 9.6-litre diesel engine, more powerful than any previously fitted to a London bus. In March 1939 the chassis was fitted with a 56-seat Chiswick-built body of a totally new design, undoubtedly the most modern yet built for a London double decker. From window pillars to step corners there were no square edges, save for the corners of the roof route number boxes which were fitted front and rear. The bus was RT 1, the forerunner of a fleet eventually totalling 7,000 buses, the largest ever built for a single operator.

RT 1 entered passenger service on route 22 (Homerton – Putney) on 9th August 1939 with war less than a month away. One hundred and fifty more RTs were built to basically the same design before the Government placed strict wartime controls on bus building and allocation. No more RTs were built for another seven years. The buses which came to the LPTB in the wartime allocation of new vehicles were almost all built to an approved Government austerity design, and mounted on Bristol, Daimler and Guy chassis. Austerity is a very appropriate description because many appeared in a dull brown or grey livery, and some even had wooden slatted seats. The graceful curves of the RT were nowhere to be seen on these buses, few concessions to aesthetic requirements being possible. But they came at a time when the ravages of war were taking a heavy toll of the London bus fleet and, with the addition of suitable refinements, they gave many years' useful service.

Chalk and cheese. The stride forward in bodywork design displayed by the RT of 1939 was dramatically reversed by the utility buses built to strict austerity standards during and immediately after the war. The example illustrated below was built in 1944 on a Daimler chassis. The last 'utilities', a batch of 'relaxed austerity' Daimlers built in 1946, were withdrawn in 1954. The RT has window netting in place, a protection against bomb blast.

Facing page In addition to over 100 buses totally written off during the war due to bomb damage, many others had to be rebodied, including LT 1231 which was badly damaged in Holborn on 8th October 1940.
Crown Copyright

Above An unidentified STL is amongst the casualties in this view at Portman Square.
Crown Copyright

Right The blackout produced many hazards and here an unsuspecting driver of one of the Green Line coaches converted to ambulances has driven into a crater made by an unexploded bomb. No patients or casualties were on board and the driver. The driver escaped with minor injuries.
Sunday Express

Peace and Standardisation

Six years of war with very little in the way of maintenance and cosmetic improvement had left London's 6,400 strong bus fleet, consisting mostly of STs, LTs and STLs, ragged and care worn. Two further years passed before the first post-war buses were delivered. Bus body building at Chiswick Works had ceased so that the plant could concentrate on overhauling, and two manufacturers, Park Royal and Weymann, were contracted to build the first batches of post-war RT buses. Delivery began in April 1947 and the first ones entered service on route 10 (Victoria – Abridge) during May. Eventually other body builders, Cravens, Leyland Motors, Metro-Cammell and Saunders Engineering, were given orders for RT family bodies to supplement those built by the two main manufacturers and keep production of RTs at maximum output.

The post-war RT strongly resembled the earlier Chiswick product except for a revised front and rear destination layout and an all-metal body construction rather than composite wood/metal, the usual Chiswick style. Gone were the rear roof number box, the sloping cab windows and the tapered rear corner panel of the pre-war model. The front roof route box disappeared on later deliveries to be replaced by a three-in-one destination display first used on the earliest STLs.

Above The first post-war RT to enter service was RT402, the first orders being split between two body builders, Park Royal and Weymann. RT402 receives admiring stares at Victoria station. S.A. Newman

Facing page The roof route number box was re-positioned to below the upper deck windows to be grouped with the destination and intermediate points blinds early in the RT's history. RT2138 shows the revised arrangement. LT Museum

The RT body construction was such that there was an almost universal interchangeability of parts. Park Royal and Weymann had been given identical specifications and between them built 5,380 of the 6,800 members of the post-war RT family, which included 2,131 Leylands. A large order was placed with Leyland for Titan PD2/1 and 2/3 chassis with 9.8-litre 115 bhp engines. These matched the power of the engine fitted to post-war RTs which was heavier (as was the body) than that in the pre-war buses. The PD2/1 chassis were fitted with standard RT bodies but classified RTL. The first batches entered service at Sidcup and West Green garages in December 1948. The 500 PD2/3s ordered were for a class of 8ft wide buses for which Leyland also built the bodies. These spacious vehicles retained the basic layout of the narrower RT and RTL buses and London Transport planned to use them on busy central London routes where the additional width in the seats and gangways would be advantageous. However, the police, wary that the extra inches might pose problems, refused to sanction the use of the RTWs in central London so they entered service in the suburbs, the first ones running on route 41 (Archway Station – Ilford) in May 1949.

The following year London Transport was allowed to conduct a series of trials designed to prove to the authorities that the RTWs did not present any undue hazards to other road users. The success of these trials led to the RTWs taking up their intended duties on trunk routes through the heart of the capital from February 1951. The 8ft wide motor bus had finally come to London.

In 1949 the 8-foot wide member of the RT family made its debut. The class, an all-Leyland product, comprised 500 buses, many of which were used in trials during 1950 to reassure the police that the operation of eight-footers in congested central London streets presented no danger to other traffic. RTW 12 is seen here working from Holloway garage on route 27A during one of the trials. It is in its original livery, which included cream upper deck window pillars, and carries a reduced route blind display. LT Museum

Above Following the unsuccessful LT 1137 of 1931, a second attempt to produce a luxury double-deck coach for Green Line services appeared in 1949 as RTC 1, a new body built on the chassis of RT 97.
Glyn Kraemer-Johnson

Above right LT's chronic bus shortage in the early post-war period was partially relieved by batches of new buses built for other operators, but diverted temporarily to London for use until new RT family buses could take their place. One such is Hants & Dorset's Bristol K6A HRU852 (TD904). It is seen in Ilford working on route 144 from West Green garage where it was based between March 1949 and April 1950. C. Carter

The post-war period was in many ways just as difficult for London Transport as the war itself had been. Britain was rebuilding, and bus construction had to take its turn in the queue for scarce materials. By 1949 bus bodies were being supplied faster than chassis, so a batch of STLs with premature body fatigue was withdrawn and the chassis modified to fit new RT bodies. Thus was born the SRT class, a well-intentioned measure which met with instant hostility from bus crews, because the smaller 7.7-litre engine in the heavier RT body made the vehicles sluggish and difficult to handle. Ultimately the SRTs were confined to work on routes without too many hills; a speedier supply of chassis by 1953 enabled them all to be withdrawn and the bodies fitted to new chassis, the last SRT running in April 1954. Just seven months later, on 11th November, the last new RT was delivered to London Transport. By that time the bus, in its familiar central bus red, country bus green and even Green Line colours had become a familiar sight in every part of the vast 1,986 square mile area served by London Transport. It had replaced almost the entire pre-war and wartime double-deck bus fleet and the 1,800 strong fleet of trams.

With the RT London Transport had gone as far as it would in achieving its time-honoured goal of a standardised bus fleet. It could take 8 to 10 years to replace a bus fleet the size of London's and technology cannot stand still all that time. By the mid-1950s more advanced double deckers were available and running for other British operators.

But in 1955 the RT reigned supreme. At the end of the year 6,170 RT/RTL/RTW buses were scheduled for service on Monday to Friday, out of a total of 7,048 vehicles; that is 87 per cent of the entire fleet.

The last half-cab single-deckers built for London Transport were the post-war T and TD classes. Weymann bodied 81 such vehicles in 1946 and Mann Egerton 130 in 1948. T 766, a Weymann bodied bus, is seen at Greenford in April 1956.
Bruce Jenkins

Classic Single-Deckers

To replace the pre-war single-deck bus fleet, including the vehicles running on the prestigious Green Line services, London Transport ordered 700 AEC Regal Mark IV chassis with Metro-Cammell bodywork. The order followed successful trials in 1950 with a Park Royal bodied AEC Regal. The new buses were classified RF, and the first entered service on Green Line route 704 (Windsor – Tunbridge Wells) in October 1951. Eventually the RFs found work on all types of London bus service from suburban red bus routes to country and Green Line routes. The class included 25 Private Hire coaches which, at 27ft 6ins long, were 2ft 6ins shorter than the majority of the class. The attractive design of the RF was very modern for its time. With their front entrance, full-fronted stylishly contoured bodies they hardly looked dated when the last ones were withdrawn in March 1979. The front entrance was a characteristic which made them eminently suitable for LT's first tentative steps into the realms of one-person operation (OPO) with large capacity buses, which began experimentally on country area route 419 (Epsom – Langley Vale) on 3rd May 1954. Ten years later history repeated itself when RFs, this time in the central area, were used to convert some red bus routes to OPO. By 1971 all the RFs remaining in service with London Transport and London Country were driver-only operated.

Bearing little relation to the pre-war members of the T class, Mann Egerton bodied T 777 is seen parked at Watford High Street garage when new in 1948. These buses lasted in service until 1962 along with the Mann Egerton TDs.
Capital Transport

In addition to the original Green Line vehicles, RFs were also produced in central and country bus versions. The basic difference between the two was that the central bus versions did not have folding entrance doors. Later, many central area RFs were used as driver-only buses and were fitted with doors. RF 365 is in its original 'doorless' form on route 254. Capital Transport

Before the minibuses of 1972, London Transport's smallest post-war buses were the 26-seater ECW bodied Guys, all 84 of which worked in the country area. One such is GS 51 seen here working on route 316. Photobus

Although the RT family, and the RFs, formed the backbone of London Transport's post-war bus fleet there were over 300 other vehicles delivered after 1945 which offered little in the way of innovation but are nevertheless worth mentioning. Between 1946 and 1948 LT took delivery of more than 200 single deckers, 80 AEC Regals and 131 Leyland PS1 Tigers. The Regals were slotted in at the end of the famous T class while the Tigers were coded TD. Weymann and Mann Egerton built the bodies for these handsome vehicles, which were to be the last open radiator single deckers delivered to London Transport. In 1950 the first of 76 AEC Regents with standard Weymann low bridge double-deck bodies was delivered. LT gave these vehicles the code RLH and they were used in both central and country bus areas until 1971. Eighty-four normal control Guy single deckers with Perkins 65bhp engines and 26-seat Eastern Coach Works bodies arrived in 1953, to replace the pre-war Leyland Cubs on the quieter driver-only operated routes in the country area.

On 1st January 1956 London's fleet of 7,000 motor buses was still in the prime of life. Even the oldest members, the 151 pre-war RTs, most of which were now being used as driver trainers, were still less than 20 years old, and the vast majority had given less than nine years' service. The award for the oldest London 'buses' still around at that time went to the 1,700 strong fleet of trolleybuses, replacement of which was high on LT's list of priorities.

RM 1 was the result of two years vigorous experimentation by the time it was photographed on route 2 in February 1956. The following July its length was increased by four inches to 27ft 4in and the radiator was repositioned from beneath the cab to the more conventional place at the front. It received a grille at the same time. *Alan B. Cross*

The Routemaster

The original intention had been to build a new fleet of trolleybuses for London and consideration was given to the possibility of a vehicle designed for construction either as a diesel bus or a trolleybus, thereby making the maximum use of interchangeable parts; surely the ultimate in standardisation! However the vehicle which was eventually unveiled as the replacement for London's trolleybuses was a stylish diesel-engined bus which London Transport christened Routemaster. The prototype was exhibited at the 1954 Commercial Motor Show.

RM 1 boasted a host of new features. For example it had no chassis. Although there had been many chassisless trolleybuses in the London fleet this was the first double-deck diesel bus built to this principle. Instead the engine and gearbox, together with the coil springs and axles, were mounted on two small subframes and were easily detachable from the 27ft long, 8ft wide Park Royal aluminium alloy body built, like the RT, with ease of maintenance and overhaul in mind. RM 1 had seats for 64 passengers instead of the customary 56, London Transport obviously having been satisfied that an extra eight would not present significant fare collection problems. To keep within legal length limitations the bus had its radiator mounted horizontally beneath the driver's cab. A plain panel, sporting the LT 'bullseye', was fitted in the position usually occupied by the radiator. In this form, it entered service on route 2 (Golders Green – Crystal Palace) on 8th February 1956. The radiator was eventually moved to its traditional position in front of the engine when the permitted maximum length was increased to 30 feet later in 1956. RM 1 was now 27ft 6ins long.

Three more prototype Routemasters were built. RM 2 had AEC running units and, like RM 1, a Park Royal body; it was painted in country area green livery. RML 3 was a Weymann bodied 9.8-litre Leyland and finally there was CRL 4, a double-deck Green Line coach with an ECW body and Leyland engine.

The production RM was generally similar in appearance to the prototypes but with a modified bonnet and radiator grille. RM 611, fresh from its first overhaul, stands in the sunshine at Aldgate Bus Station in June 1965 on the busy 253 route from Holloway garage.

The first production RMs entered service on selected busy central London routes during the summer of 1959. They were withdrawn later in the year to reappear on 11th November at Poplar and West Ham garages in their intended role as trolleybus replacements, a function they performed until May 1962 when London's last trolleybuses were withdrawn. After that the class made considerable inroads into the Leyland members of the RT family.

The RCLs, built in 1965 exclusively for Green Line services, represented the ultimate in comfort for passengers, but within ten years they had nearly all been demoted to ordinary bus work as crew operation on even the busiest Green Line services was becoming uneconomic. RCL 2218, the first of the 43-strong batch, drives past sister vehicle RCL 2227 in Aldgate Bus Station. Although working different routes both buses were allocated to Romford garage, which was to operate buses of this type until January 1972. *Capital Transport*

All the standard RMs were painted red, RM 2's brief spell in country bus green during 1957 being the only exception. The body-building contract for the Routemaster had been given exclusively to Park Royal, and in the ten years between 1958 and 1968 the firm built 2,821 bodies for London Transport, mostly of the standard 64-seat variety. However there were variants. In 1961 twenty-four 30ft-long 72-seater Routemasters were built, easily distinguishable from the standard RM by the addition of a small window in the centre of each deck. The RMLs, as they were eventually classified, were the forerunners of a further 500 delivered between 1965 and 1968 for the central and country areas.

Following successful trials with the Green Line coach Routemaster, CRL 4, London Transport ordered a batch of 68 coach RMs (coded RMC) in 1962. For the first time Green Line had a fleet of double-deck vehicles, offering high standards in comfort, standards taken still further in 1965 with the delivery of forty-three 30ft long coach Routemasters (RCLs). There was also a forward entrance 30ft Routemaster (RMF 1254) which was used as the prototype of a fleet of 65 coaches to run the BEA service in place of the AEC Regals. These were delivered in 1966/67.

In 1966 London Transport produced its last own-design bus, the FRM, a front-entrance, rear-engined version of the Routemaster. By then the signals were clear: London's 'bus of the future' would be one without the traditional conductor; but with several generations of successful buses behind it London Transport considered itself more than capable of designing a suitable rear-engined bus for one-man operation. The prototype FRM had an AEC AV 961 rear-mounted engine. Its 72-seat Park Royal body contained about 60 per cent of standard RM body parts so a large class of FRMs would have co-existed happily with their open-platform contemporaries. But it was not to be. By the time FRM 1 entered service from Tottenham garage on 26th June 1967, London Transport had already placed an order for 150 single-deck buses of manufacturer's standard design to satisfy the urgent need to start conversions to one-manning, and more were to follow. When these were ordered, one-man operation of double deckers was not permitted.

On 1st March 1968, without ceremony, brand new RML 2760 entered service from Upton Park garage. Not only was it the last Routemaster of all, it was also the last London bus to be built with a traditional open rear platform.

RF 694 glides through the Buckinghamshire countryside on route 316 in August 1965. It is still in its original Lincoln green and cream country bus livery, but is now one-man operated. In January 1970 it passed to London Country Bus Services, along with the rest of London Transport's country area and Green Line fleet. It did not have a long existence with its new owner however, as it was withdrawn in June 1972, almost seven years before the last LCBS RF was withdrawn.
Alan Mortimer

Pay As You Enter

The use of driver-only buses in London can be traced right back to horse bus days, but until the 1960s they were confined to the quietest routes. The problems which led London Transport to introduce large-scale driver only operation have their origins as far back as 1950 with the ending of post-war petrol rationing. Sales of private cars increased sharply, with a consequent fall in the number of people relying exclusively on buses for work and leisure travel. The resulting drop in revenue made it difficult for LT to keep its wage rates competitive with those being offered in other industries where unsocial hours, an unfortunate but essential element of jobs in public transport, were not part of the working conditions. Staff, attracted by better prospects elsewhere, left in their hundreds. While there was some fluctuation in staff shortages year by year during the 1950s, some idea of the situation can be gathered from London Transport's Annual Report for 1959 which recorded that the staff shortages for the road services operating department rose from 828 at the end of 1958 to 2,785 at the end of 1959. The total number of drivers and conductors employed dropped by 9 per cent from 39,874 to 36,303, partly because of the increased vacancies and partly due to the service cuts following the 1958 bus strike. As reliability suffered, more people took to their cars: the number of cars coming into central London during the morning rush hour more than doubled between 1952 and 1964 to 66,000.

In 1966 London Transport published a report entitled 'Reshaping London's Bus Services' which set out plans for radical changes to the structure of London's bus routes, including the introduction of a large fleet of driver-only buses to lead the front line attack against staff shortages. Routes were to be shorter and some would be operated on a flat-fare principle. All major centres in Greater London would have a network of flat-fare 'satellite' routes operated by large capacity single-deck buses equipped for automatic fare collection.

The previous year, London Transport had ordered 58 double deckers with standard Park Royal front entrance bodywork, similar to buses then running in many provincial towns. Fifty of the buses had Leyland Atlantean 11.1-litre engines. They were painted red, coded XA and used in trials alongside new RMLs on routes 24 and 76 to compare the operation of doored and open-platform vehicles on busy routes. The remaining eight were Daimler Fleetline (XF class)

In 1966 London Transport bought eight front-entrance Park Royal bodied Daimler Fleetlines, primarily for use in the country area, but initially for comparison tests with the Leyland Atlantean version of the same bus and standard RMLs. It is on one of these tests on central area route 271 that XF 7, originally allocated to East Grinstead garage, is seen. LT engineers decided that the Fleetline was most suitable for the Board's needs and the DMS was the result. Capital Transport

buses painted green and fitted with Gardner 6LX 10.4-litre engines. They were allocated to East Grinstead garage's route 424 and were used as normal crew-operated buses for most of the day. At that time legislation did not permit the operation of double-deck buses by just one person. However after the evening rush hour the upper deck was closed off and the XFs became nocturnal driver only single deckers.

The other significant development was the introduction of route 500, a flat-fare express route linking Victoria Station with Marble Arch and Oxford Street for commuters and shoppers travelling from one of London's busiest main line rail terminals to one of the principal shopping and business thoroughfares in the capital. Passengers deposited 6d pieces (2½p) in new style coin-in-the-slot machines to gain entrance; no tickets were issued.

Route 500 was given the name 'Red Arrow'. To run it London Transport purchased 14 Strachans-bodied AEC AH691 Swifts, which LT christened 'Merlin' and coded XMS. They were designed to move large numbers of short distance riders at busy times and had a carrying capacity of 73 (25 seated and 48 standing). Those who ventured aboard route 500 did not seem to find the experience too arduous, the service being hailed as an unqualified success. The 500 was the first route in a network of 'Red Arrows' centred on London's principal main line railway termini.

XMS 3 loads up at Victoria station on the first day of Red Arrow route 500, 18th April 1966. In rush hours, most of its passengers would have to stand, and the official standing capacity of 48 was sometimes exceeded. In the background part of the bus station is temporarily occupied by building work for the Victoria Line.

London Transport seemed satisfied with the Merlins, for in 1967 it placed large orders for similar buses, this time with Metro-Cammell Weymann bodywork, for use in the initial stages of its mammoth Bus Reshaping Programme. Eventually 665 were delivered with quantities for central and country area routes.

The first MBs, as the class was collectively called, arrived in the autumn of 1967. The buses were divided into sub-groups depending on their eventual use. The standard MB came in two versions, one with a 45-seat front entrance, centre exit body, and the other with a 50-seat front entrance/exit layout.

The MBs were for use on conventional services converted to driver-only. The other two classes, coded MBA and MBS, had front entrance, centre exit bodies with room for 25 seated passengers and standing area for 48. The MBAs were designed for Red Arrow work and were fitted with slot machines and turnstiles. The MBSs were intended for London Transport's new central area suburban flat fare 'standee' services and the 'Autofare' routes in the country area which were to operate with graduated fares. They were all fitted with automatic fare collection machines so passengers could serve themselves. LT was anxious to tailor its new buses to the task they were expected to perform and was determined that the new style services were not going to cause more problems than they solved.

Shorter versions (33ft 5ins) of the MBs and MBSs entered service in 1970 following problems with the 36-footers. These were the AEC Swifts. Although more manoeuvrable than the Merlins they proved just as mechanically unreliable, a feature which resulted in all having been withdrawn, mostly for scrap, by February 1981. SMS 82 entered service at Edgware garage in June 1970 and, as SMD 82, was withdrawn exactly seven years later following conversion to a single-door entrance/exit vehicle. Capital Transport

But things did not go as smoothly as planned. Protracted negotiations with the Trade Unions over the introduction of driver-only buses caused the postponement of the first 'area' schemes planned for introduction in April 1968. It was not until September that Bus Reshaping finally got under way with the introduction of new service pattern networks in Walthamstow and Wood Green. In the months that followed similar 'area' schemes, began in Ealing, Stratford and Peckham, among others, with routes elsewhere being converted piecemeal.

Far from solving problems the new buses actually added to them. The popularity of the Red Arrows was not shared by their suburban counterparts. Despite an intensive publicity campaign there were delays at stops while passengers fumbled for the right money and the 'serve yourself' ticket machines were unreliable. Having got past all that, many weary passengers could not find a vacant seat. All this made the new-style services slow and unpopular. Moreover the Merlins did not prove sufficiently robust for the work they had to do in London and their 36ft length caused problems in narrow and congested streets which had presented no difficulty to the shorter RT/RM buses they replaced. For its next large bus order London Transport opted for the shorter (33ft 5ins) AEC Swift, 838 of which were eventually acquired. As with the MBs there were sub-divisions of Swifts. The SM class were front entrance/exit 42-seater buses for the central bus area, while the bulk of the class (coded SMS) had front entrances and centre exits and could carry 67 passengers (33 seated and 34 standing). The body building for the SM family was shared by Marshalls of Cambridge, Metro-Cammell and Park Royal. All had AEC 505 132bhp engines.

The Swifts also proved to be mechanically unreliable. Moreover, the root cause of the whole exercise, staff shortage, was still affecting service reliability. It was a bleak time for London Transport, and rather a sad note on which to end its long, happy and eventful association with AEC, which finished with the delivery of the last SMS in March 1972. By this time AEC was part of British Leyland, which proceeded gradually to phase out the use of the AEC marque. On 25th May 1979 Leyland finally shut down the AEC factory at Southall where countless chassis for London buses had been built, thereby closing one of the most significant chapters in London bus history.

Upstairs Regained

In 1967 restrictions on the operation of driver-only double-deck buses had been lifted. This came too late for London Transport which had outstanding orders for several hundred single deckers, each with carrying capacities equal to or in excess of its RT and RM buses.

However, in November 1969, route 233 (West Croydon – Roundshaw) was converted from one-man RF to one-man XA. The 233 schedule required only one bus, but this conversion provides another entry for our extensive log of London bus 'firsts' because the 233 was the first London route to be operated by a driver-only double decker. The XAs were used on a new Croydon flat-fare network the following April, by which time LT had ordered 17 Daimler Fleetlines with Park Royal bodies for delivery later in the year. Before the first one arrived the order had been increased by a further 100, London Transport nailing its colours in support of the double decker firmly to the mast.

The first two of the new Fleetlines were exhibited at the 1970 Commercial Motor Show, and from the type's debut on routes 95 and 220 on 2nd January 1971 the DMS gradually became a familiar sight all over London, not just on the RT/RM routes converted to opo, but also on the capacity-strained single-deck services converted back to double-deck.

The Fleetlines were powered by Gardner 6LXB 10.45-litre engines, and the body building for the class was shared by Park Royal and Metro-Cammell. With new 89-passenger DMSs being used to replace the unreliable MB/SM buses, the opo conversion programme slowed down. Another factor in this was the recognition that the busiest central London routes would need to retain crew operation for the foreseeable future. A batch of Fleetlines was therefore built especially for crew operation and enabled withdrawal of RTs without increasing overall the level of driver-only operation in the fleet. The Merlins and Swifts were sold, mostly for scrap, many being broken up alongside life-expired RTs twenty years their senior.

The last batch of DMSs delivered in 1976–77 were designed to be quieter than the rest of the class and had a modified engine shroud. These were known as the B20 DMSs. Most of the earlier members of the class were sold in the early 1980s, many for service elsewhere. Some even returned to London bus routes sporting the liveries of other operators working routes under contract for London Transport.

The last DMSs in regular London Buses service were withdrawn at the end of 1992.

An early route to be converted from RM operation to double-deck one-man operation was the 271. A Park Royal bodied DMS is seen in Holloway.
Capital Transport

London's Buses in the Seventies and Eighties

The 1968 Transport Act nationalised much of Britain's non-municipal bus network by setting up the National Bus Company (NBC); it also gave the Minister of Transport powers to make grants available for, among other things, the purchase of buses. The Transport (London) Act 1969 vested London Transport's country and Green Line coach services in a new NBC subsidiary company, London Country Bus Services Ltd, while red bus services and the Underground, remaining as London Transport, came under the financial and broad policy control of the Greater London Council. The 14 years under the GLC were certainly among the most eventful for London's buses. London Transport was well and truly in the political arena, with fares and service levels prominent issues in elections for the governing power at County Hall.

London's bus engineers have always been anxious to test new vehicle concepts as they were developed, and the Experimental shop at Chiswick Works often concealed a new chassis or even a complete bus acquired for close examination. Sometimes the vehicles actually found their way into passenger service so they could be tested under 'field' conditions. No longer producing its own buses, despite an abortive attempt at a new design in the mid-1970s, LT had to know the potential of the buses which were available in an ever-developing market.

When the order for Swifts was completed 12 new single deckers of two new designs were purchased, six Metro-Scanias and six Leyland Nationals, an example of the former having been tried out in 1970 and the latter being Leyland's newly-developed and appropriately named standard single decker which, by 1973 when the LT order was delivered, was becoming a common sight nationwide. London Transport had ordered the 10-metre version of the National and, apart from the standard LT seat moquette and the familiar red livery, there was little to distinguish the six from the hundreds of others running up and down the country. By 1981 Leyland Nationals had replaced all the remaining Merlins and Swifts on the routes which London Transport had decided would remain single-deck, and the Mark II version had exclusive control of the Red Arrow network. Like the RMLs, many Mark II Nationals have undergone something of a transformation, being modernised with completely new body styling under the National Greenway project.

Below left Following the trials of the Metro Scania single-deckers, London Transport purchased 164 of the double-deck versions. These buses, named Metropolitans, entered service on central London trunk routes in 1976. They later moved to opo work in south east London. MD 11 is seen in Edgware Road near Marble Arch. Capital Transport

Below right An early result of the Leyland/LT co-operation in bus design was the Titan. NHG 732P was one of two prototypes which underwent extensive trials in London, mainly on route 24 from Chalk Farm garage. It is seen here working on route 3. The Titans, with their 66-seat (five fewer than the Metrobus) Park Royal bodies powered by Gardner QXB engines, were delivered at the same time as the Metrobuses although each type was confined to separate operating divisions. Capital Transport

In 1977 Metro-Cammell took their Anglo-Swedish 'Metropolitan' double-decker to its next stage and produced an all-British version which it named 'Metrobus'. LT had taken 164 Metropolitans and ordered five of the new Metrobus as an initial batch, the first, coded MT 1, being delivered in April 1978. The production batch, delivery of which began with M 6 in February 1979, had a single aperture two-piece display, the route number and the via points now being on the same blind with the ultimate destination displayed below.

Meanwhile Leyland, in consultation with London Transport, had developed a bus especially suited to London conditions but with a market potential elsewhere. Leyland called the project B15 and the designers resurrected some of the features of the FRM. A plywood mock-up was constructed in 1973 and a small batch of prototypes was built and made available for trial in 1975. LT tested two of the prototypes, which were given the name 'Titan', between 1975 and 1978, using them on crew-operated route 24 (Hampstead Heath – Pimlico) before placing an order for 250 buses.

The first production Titans (T class) were delivered in August 1978 and, following the customary period of staff familiarisation and training, they entered service the following December on routes from Hornchurch garage, just as the first single deckers bearing the same famous class code had done exactly 49 years earlier.

Unhappily the Titan was dogged by the bad fortune which had been hovering around London's buses for many years. Production was hardly under way when Leyland announced that it was shutting down the Park Royal factory in west

Metrobus M 78 is in the standard livery in which the bulk of the 1440-strong class of standard Ms was delivered. Behind can be seen a bus from an earlier delivery with the white top-deck window surround, a much more attractive feature which had adorned the later DMSs as well as the first Titans and Metrobuses. Geoff Rixon

As RF replacement drew near, 95 Bristol LH6L single deckers powered by Leyland 125bhp engines with 39-seat Eastern Coach Works bodies were purchased for the routes where the operation of the larger Leyland Nationals might have caused problems. The BLs were only 7ft 6ins wide, the narrowest London buses since the RT. There were also 17 of a shorter version, coded BS, which LT found useful on some routes originally introduced with minibuses.

London. The factory had been building London bus bodies since the 1930s and it finally closed in 1981 after the initial order for 250 Ts had been completed. Leyland transferred Titan production to its Workington plant, but the move north caused a lengthy interruption to deliveries. By December 1981 there were only 370 Ts in the fleet, against 700 Metrobuses. Although the Titan was proving reliable in London service, Leyland were disappointed with orders from elsewhere, an important factor if the bus was to remain in production. The company announced in 1983 that Titan production was to cease, which it did following the delivery of T 1125 in November 1984. At about the same time MCW introduced a Mark II version of the Metrobus and began to phase out production of the Mark I type, which ceased on completion of the LT order with M 1440 in January 1986.

London Buses' last major purchases consisted of 259 Eastern Coachworks bodied Leyland Olympians delivered between 1984 and 1987. Most of them could be found south of the river, including L41 at work from Sidcup garage. Many still survive with Arriva in south London. The bulk of those which were transferred to Stagecoach have been sold. *Ramon Hefford*

The Leyland Olympian was the bus designed as the replacement for the Bristol VRT, the standard National Bus Company double decker. At a glance the Olympian strongly resembles the Titan but there are many differences, one being that the Olympian (L class) is two inches shorter in height at 14ft 2½ins. Olympians seat 75 passengers as against the 66-seater Titans, but they have in common the fact that they are powered by the Gardner QXB engine. They formed the only bulk order placed after the establishment of LRT in June 1984. The last of this batch of Leyland Olympians arrived in January 1987. The Olympian fleet was later increased by the addition of further batches, and at the beginning of the year 2000 there were more Olympians in London service than any other single type of double decker.

Tendered Routes

When London Buses Ltd was created in 1984 as a subsidiary of London Regional Transport it inherited a virtual operating monopoly of London's bus routes. But the days of a monolithic bus operator for London were effectively over, for the first invitations to tender for selected routes had already been made. London Buses had to take its place in the arena of competition and free enterprise.

The aim of bus route tendering is to make services more efficient and reduce the level of subsidy which the government has to pay in grants. In 1983, its last full year of financial control over London Transport, the Greater London Council contributed a subsidy of £220 million to help run London's buses and the Underground. One of the objectives under the 1984 LRT Act was to reduce the subsidy level by securing the best and most cost-effective services. An initial batch of twelve bus routes was put out to tender in October 1984 and the successful contractors commenced operation the following July.

The tendering process involves prospective contractors submitting a detailed profile of their company, including financial status and available resources, to LRT along with their tender bid. The tender invitations give prospective operators a full service specification drawn up by LRT planners, including duration of the service each day and minimum number of journeys to be operated etc. The choice of vehicle is left to the operator, subject to guidelines from LRT on capacity, destination displays and other detailed design features.

Above Scancoaches was an early independent operator onto the London bus route scene when it successfully tendered to operate route 283 in 1986. For this they bought five Scania K92CRBs with 47-seater Jonckheere bodywork bringing a little bit of Scandinavia to inner west London for a few years until June 1989 when the route passed to London United. The five coaches, including C352 SVV seen here, were bought by Smiths of Alcester.

The Midibus Revolution

New in 1989/90 were 57 Dennis Dart 8.5 SDLs with bodywork by Duple and Carlyle. They were followed in 1991 by 110 more. The bulk of them worked for the London United subsidiary of LBL, as did DT19 seen here bound for Richmond on the H22.

The route restructuring and local networking which has been a prominent feature of LRT's competitive tendering process has brought a host of new faces to the London bus scene. These are the midi- and mini-buses which have become a familiar sight not just around London, but right in the centre as well.

What are today called minibuses and midibuses can be traced right back to Shillibeer's original Omnibus of 1829. Small buses have traditionally been used in the outer suburbs and in London Transport's former country area. Twenty-seater Leyland Cubs were purchased in the 1930s, in both front- and rear-engined versions. In the 1950s, the choice was the 26-seater Guy Vixen. Bristol LHs were bought in the 1970s, both by London Transport and London Country.

Today's breed of midibus is much more numerous and widespread, though in recent years there has been a move towards longer single-deckers (typically seating 34–40 passengers) on routes previously operated with 26–30 seaters. The main supplier is Dennis Vehicles, which has provided over 2,500 of its Dart chassis in various versions. Other well known makers include Mercedes-Benz, Renault, Fiat and Metro-Cammell. Bodywork comes from a variety of sources.

The Later LBL Years

In the years between 1987 and privatisation in 1994 far fewer new double deckers were delivered for service in London than at any other time since 1970. Just 198 out of the total number of double deckers in service with LBL at the end of 1994 were delivered since L 263, the last of the main batch of Leyland Olympians, arrived in January 1987.

Single-deck fortunes revived after LT's rather unhappy flirtation with large capacity single-deckers on busy routes in the late 60s and early 70s. In the late 1980s, when the original batches of Leyland Nationals became due for replacement, the LBL units were given powers to order new buses providing their submissions were approved by the Company's financial management. Several unique vehicles were obtained for evaluation in the early 1990s prior to orders being placed, including two Renault PR1002s, both with 51-seater Northern Counties bodies, one of which was purchased and coded RN 1. Others included a DAF Bendibus loaned from South Yorkshire Transport, and a couple of Optare/DAF Deltas, a trial which resulted in orders eventually totalling 53 (class DA) powered by DAF's LC 1160 11.6 litre engine. The DAs were delivered in a very attractive silver livery which was not perpetuated on subsequent single deck deliveries like the LA, LN and VN classes which made their debut on busy central London routes in 1992/93. The LAs were 16 Alexander bodied Dennis Lances with Cummins 6CT8 engines. Similar chassis and engines to those on the LAs powered the 31 LNs, the only difference being the 37-seater Northern Counties bodywork. The LNs arrived in 1993. The VNs, which were delivered in 1993, had 40-seater Northern Counties bodies mounted on Volvo B10B55 chassis, and were used for a time exclusively on route 88.

Conversion of routes from double-deck to single-deck has been found to create capacity problems at times, and some routes have reverted to double-deck operation. Between 1993 and 1997 these Volvo 37-seaters operated the 88 route.
Capital Transport

A sense of tradition no doubt led LT Buses to number the route 207 express service from Shepherd's Bush to Uxbridge 607, as this was the route number of the trolleybus service which plied the Uxbridge Road until 1960. The new 607 uses low-floor Dennis Darts with Wright Pathfinder bodywork. Paul Weston

The underlying trend in single-deck bus design as the 1990s gathered pace was accessibility and at the forefront of single-deck deliveries since 1994 has been the low-floor bus in the form of chassis by Dennis (the Lance SLF11SDA) and Scania (N113CRL). These dual door vehicles carry between 31 and 39 passengers and most have bodywork by Wrights of Ballymena, or Plaxton.

Since the early 1990s, Dennis has attained the lion's share of the London midi-bus market, and examples of vehicles based on variations of its popular Dart chassis can be found in service with almost every London bus operator, not least those descended from the former LBL units. Early London Darts had bodywork by Wrights of Ballymena and Carlyle, but by the end of the 1990s the most popular bodywork for the Dart was the 'Pointer' from Plaxton.

Even smaller buses found a niche in the London scene in the 1980s and early 90s. The route restructuring and local networking, which was a prominent feature of the early tendering exercises, brought small capacity mini-buses to the suburbs in a big way. These were based on a variety of chassis, from Renault and Mercedes-Benz to Volkswagen, but many of these mini pioneers have since given way to larger capacity midi-buses.

Capital Citybus is a key player in the London bus scene in north east and east London. The company, now part of the First Group, owns buses of many different types, some new and some bought from other UK operators. A 33-seater Optare Excel L1000 was photographed at Ilford Broadway.
Capital Transport

The Privatisation Era

In 1994 the operating subsidiaries which had made up London Buses Ltd passed to the private sector. London had been seen as a special case when the main thrust of bus deregulation took place and, as such, had not been included, although it was still Government policy that one-day London's bus services would be deregulated as well. In November 1993 the Government thought again, and announced a deferment of its plans to deregulate London's buses, which had been scheduled for late 1994. The announcement assured the role of London Transport as custodian and planner of London's bus services, at least for the foreseeable future. However the sale of the London Buses subsidiary units, deemed essential if all the operators of London's bus routes were to enjoy the commercial freedoms of the private sector operators who were now running a significant proportion of London's buses, went ahead and all the respective companies were in the hands of their new owners by the end of that year.

The new owners were an interesting mixture of management and company buy-outs, and many organisations which had emerged as key players during the first ten years since Britain's bus industry was deregulated, were eager to grab a slice of the country's most lucrative bus market. The successful bidders were:

Cowie Group plc (Leaside and South London)
Go Ahead Group (London Central)
MTL Trust Holdings (London Northern)
Stagecoach Holdings (East London and Selkent)

Management team buyouts took place at:

CentreWest   London General   London United
Metroline   Westlink

Following the sell-off, a new division, London Transport Buses, was created to plan and procure London's extensive network of bus routes, with the newly privatised former LBL segments taking the lion's share of the tenders. LT Buses was also charged with promoting bus travel and managing the infrastructure which went to make up efficient bus operation in the form of bus stations, stands, shelters and stops.

Most of the Routemasters remaining in service today are owned by the privatised London companies. The Go-Ahead Group own those used on route 36 and a refurbishment programme was begun for its RMs in the summer of 2000. RM 1033 is seen in Peckham.
Capital Transport

London's Buses in the New World

Since the sale of the former LBL units the double-decker has seen something of a revival, and the single-decker has gone from strength to strength. Although 1994 was a bleak year with no new 'deckers' being purchased by the new owners of the former red bus companies, the years between 1995 and 2000 told a different story. New bus purchases are made not only to upgrade existing fleets, but also to work on routes newly gained on tender. Bus manufacturing too has undergone something of a revolution and London can no longer boast of having a unique bus fleet tailor-made for its unusual operating conditions. With the exception of the Routemaster, 600 examples of which were in service at the end of June 2000, most of the buses found working London routes today can be seen in any town and city in the UK. Such variety has not been seen since the independent era of the 1920s.

Today's principal chassis builders are DAF, Dennis, Mercedes-Benz, Optare, Scania and Volvo. Double-deck bodies come principally from Alexander, Northern Counties and Plaxton. These three also supply single-deck bodies along with East Lancs, Marshall, Optare and Wright. Between 1994 and 1998 buses from all these manufacturers became a familiar sight in and around London working with the operators of the former LBL units and other independent companies which have tendered successfully for bus route work.

The Disability Discrimination Act (1995) was introduced to facilitate greater ease of movement for disabled and wheelchair bound people. It has influenced

Plaxton has scored considerable success with its low-floor President body, which can be found either on Dennis Trident or Volvo B7L chassis with many London bus route operators, including Arriva, Metroline, London Central and General, and the First Group. First Capital have 87 of the 9.9 metre version, which seat 59. These can be found principally on routes 1 and 25 and on several routes in the Walthamstow area, including the 97, on which No.862 was photographed in July 2000.
Colin Brown

Devoid of any external advertising and with its Alexander ALX 400 body gleaming in the sunshine, brand new Arriva London Dennis Trident DLA 195 had only a few miles on the clock when it was photographed at Northumberland Park in July 2000. Almost all the operators of London bus routes now have variations of Alexander's ALX low-floor double-deckers in their fleets. Colin Brown

bus safety and design by stipulating that all new buses must be wheelchair accessible. By the start of 1998 the first double-deck buses to conform to the requirements of the Act were coming off the production lines. All the big manufacturers are in the process of developing chassis to meet the new guidelines on accessibility. Dennis has the Trident; DAF and Volvo have similar low-floor models.

Although London Transport Buses was not a bus operator in the true sense, it awarded a significant proportion of its route contracts on the basis that new vehicles would be operated. To this end it set out to influence the best in design, catering for the needs of all bus passengers, especially young mothers with children, the elderly and disabled. The results of a wide-ranging study into future double-deck bus design undertaken in 1996 were manifested in the new generation of low floor double-deckers, which began to arrive during 1998. They embodied many features then commonplace on new low-floor single-deckers including of course reduced fuel emissions.

LT Buses role as a protagonist was welcomed by London's key bus operators and the organisation was actively involved with major bus manufacturers on key elements of new bus design. In this way London's legions of daily bus travellers could rest assured that a centralised overseeing body still played an active part in design and comfort. A landmark was passed early in 2000 when the two-thousandth low-floor bus joined the London fleet.

Into the 21st Century

Much has changed since privatisation of London's buses came on the scene in 1994. During the latter 1990s a number of mergers and sell-offs took place resulting in a slightly different picture by the year 2000. Some of these changes reflected events nationally, with the emergence of big players such as Arriva (Cowie Group) and First Group to join the more established organisations like Stagecoach. Some former 'independent' companies are now within the folds of large operators. Grey Green is part of Arriva London, and First Group owns Capital Citybus.

In March 2000 London Transport became a bus operator once more when the contract company Harris Bus went into receivership. In the absence of an alternative contractor to take over the running of the five LTB routes contracted to Harris Bus, London Buses Limited, using the operating name East Thames Buses, was recreated to take them over. The Harris Bus vehicles, 43 double-deckers and 23 single-deckers, were taken over as well, LBL maintaining the Harris Bus depot in Belvedere as the operating base for routes 108, 132, 180 and 661, but moving back into Ash Grove garage to operate the routes in north east London (128, 129 and 150). Gradually the distinctive lime-green and blue Harris Bus livery gave way to the traditional London red.

An even bigger change took place on 3rd July 2000 when London Transport Buses and LBL, along with Tramlink, London River Services, Victoria Coach station, the latter all LT subsidiaries, joined the Docklands Light Railway, the Public Carriage Office and London Street Management under the Transport for London (T/L) umbrella. T/L was now the overall planning authority for almost all London's transport; the Underground was to come on board in 2001. Under this huge shake-up LTB became London Bus Services, but its role as planner and influential force for London's bus services continues.

Almost full circle – as the East Thames Buses logo seems to suggest. This company was set up following the collapse of Harris Bus and is owned and run by London Bus Services, a subsidiary of Transport for London. Publicly owned buses have returned, albeit in a small way.

Bus Usage

Popular images of London in the rush hour usually feature people crowding onto tube trains or fighting their way out of crowded stations. However, far more people ride on London's buses each day than travel by tube, but over past decades the number has seen some quite marked fluctuations. In 1934, the number of journeys made by bus in the LPTB (London Transport) area, including country buses and Green Line coaches, was 1,950,000,000. The figure continued to rise, hitting a pre-war peak of 2,223 billion in 1938/39. A natural decline during the war was reversed in the late forties when bus usage rose to even higher levels, peaking at 2,746 billion in 1949, a year when the figure for the Underground was 703 million. The decline began during the 1950s. The 1955 figure of 2,737 billion was the last healthy year.

A lot was happening to reduce the need for bus travel, particularly for leisure. Between 1950 and 1960 private car ownership in the London Transport area increased by 250 per cent. The little box with its flickering images in the corner of the living room was a good reason for many not to go out for the evening. The start of commercial television in the London area in 1955 increased further the choice of entertainment. Cinemas and theatres closed and leisure bus travel declined.

As buses ran empty during off-peak periods and less revenue was earned, LT could not keep its wage rates competitive. Staff left for better paid jobs in other industries and service reliability began to suffer as staff shortages began to bite. A crippling seven-week bus strike in 1958 prompted even more bus users to invest in their own transport. In 1959 the number of passenger journeys on London's buses was 2,281 billion, a figure 10% below the 1957 total despite being slightly inflated by the inclusion of journeys made on trolleybus routes converted to bus. The decline continued unabated during the 1960s, with 1,786 billion journeys being made in 1969, the last year they included country area and Green Line buses.

In the new GLC dominated era of the 1970s and early 80s things fared little better as many of LT's attempts at improving service reliability failed to bring the desired results. Also people's travel habits changed. No longer would housewives take the bus to go to the shops. Not only were more women going out to work, even those who stayed at home preferred a weekly shop, taking the hatchback to the local out-of-town superstore instead of the traditional bus ride to the local shopping centre two or three times a week. The family hatchback was also used for the twice daily 'school run', taking more custom away from the buses. Although these shifts in travel patterns were not universal, they did have some detrimental effect on bus usage. The decline in bus travellers thus continued virtually year on year right through to 1995. In 1996/97 1,234 billion journeys were made on London's buses, the following year it was 1,277 billion. A dip of 10 billion for 1998/99 was redressed for 1999/2000 when the figure rose to 1,296 billion. It remains to be seen whether London Bus Services Ltd is able to maintain this happy trend through the many initiatives it has to improve the range and reliability of its services.

Following the 1958 bus strike, London Transport mounted a big publicity campaign to attract people back to buses who had got out of the habit of using them. 'Hop on a Bus' was a slogan that had been used previously by London Transport in 1937.

Appendix I: Ticketing

Early in the history of London's buses, conductors marked on a form the number of passengers that had travelled on their buses during particular spells of duty. They then paid in a corresponding sum in takings. A regular check was made by plain clothes inspectors. The LGOC maintained its counting system for many years, seemingly in the full knowledge that it was being abused by staff, who had to be careful not to pay in too little in takings for fear of arousing suspicion. The practice, and the half hearted way the General tried to remedy it, was a source of annoyance to the company's shareholders, who no doubt took great interest in the ticket-issuing system introduced by London Road Car when it started business in 1881. Road Car used a system of numbered tickets which enabled a more accurate check to be kept on fares paid. Later the Bell Punch ticket machine was used by the company to validate tickets for specific journeys and by 1890 the Bell Punch system was being used by many bus and tram operators except the General and its associates. It seems that the General only took positive steps to adopt an all-ticket system after it had been approached with the idea of selling advertising space on the ticket backs. In 1891 the company decided to adopt the Bell Punch system, implementing it on 31st May after having first increased staff wages to avoid a dispute. This was to no avail because the General's crews did strike, from 6th June, bringing out the staff of most of the other bus companies, including Road Car, in the process. The strike lasted a week and is noteworthy not just in that it ushered in an era of better staff conditions, but it was also one of the first strikes involving a Trade Union.

Very soon conductors with a rack of Bell Punch tickets to hand and cancelling machines strapped to their tunics became a familiar sight on London's road transport and were to remain so for more than half a century. In the heyday of the Bell Punch, 4,000 million tickets were printed each year.

The Bell Punch survived several attempts to supersede it until 1953, when the Gibson ticket machine, designed by George Gibson, former Superintendent at London Transport's Effra Road ticket machine works, made its appearance.

The Gibson carried a single roll of paper on which could be printed a variety of different ticket denominations just by turning a wheel on the side of the machine to the appropriate fare. A built-in meter recorded the number and types of tickets issued. It took five years for the Bell Punch machines to be replaced, the last ones remaining in use at West Ham and Poplar trolleybus depots until October 1958.

The Gibson was not the only ticket machine to supersede the Bell Punch. Conductors on Green Line coaches used a machine called a Setright which was also based on the ticket roll principle.

When London Transport began converting some of its country area routes to driver-only operation in the 1950s another new style of ticket machine was adopted. This was the Ultimate, a machine capable of issuing six different denominations of pre-printed ticket with considerable ease. Ultimates were also used on the central area RF buses on driver-only services from 1964.

In 1967 London Transport introduced another new machine, the Almex, which could be used by either conductors or driver/operators. The tickets issued from the Almex were smaller than those issued by the Gibson, so

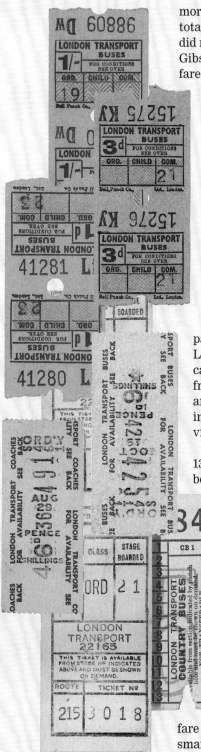

more tickets could be produced per roll. The Almex also made the job of totalling up the cash simpler by having a wider fare range so that conductors did not have to issue a combination of tickets for higher fare values as with the Gibson. The Almex contained a cassette which recorded up to 4,000 different fare transactions. It was thought that the information contained on the cassettes would also be of value in collating information about passenger travel patterns.

The Almex became the standard ticket machine when one-person operation was introduced on a large scale in the 1970s. Today's driver/operators also use a sophisticated computer-based machine called Wayfarer, perched on the corner of the cab area. The tickets issued by a Wayfarer give considerably more information than has previously been seen on bus tickets, including the date and time of issue, together with the garage code and running number of the bus involved.

In October 1992 Wayfarer's new 'Clipper' electronic ticket machine was introduced on crew buses as a replacement for the Gibson. As an ominous sign of the times, the Clipper incorporates a personal alarm and, with the future very much in mind, can read Smartcards. Within the year Clippers had all but replaced the Gibson, the last examples of which were withdrawn from Westbourne Park garage in October 1993.

Smartcard technology, or stored value ticketing, whereby bus passengers pay for bus travel in advance at selected ticket agents, was tried out on London's buses in a trial based in the Harrow area from February 1994. Credit card sized Smartcards containing a tiny silicon chip could be "read" in a fraction of a second by special cardreaders fitted to 200 buses in the Harrow area. The system offered top security. The holder's photograph was lasered into the card along with personal information and a code word which made it virtually impossible to use one fraudulently.

Early in 1997, following trials with modified Clipper machines on routes 137 and 159, passengers on crew-operated buses were issued with tickets bearing the destination to which the fare they had paid was valid, thereby diminishing the likelihood of overriding disputes arising between passengers and conductors. Between 1998/99 a new electronic ticket machine was introduced on London's driver-only buses. Made by Wayfarer it too details the last fare stage for which the ticket was valid as well as displaying an electronic version of the route fare chart to assist the driver. The new machines can be modified to read and accept Smart stored value tickets.

In 1998 London Transport launched its PRESTIGE project to plan and implement a revolution in ticketing on buses and the Underground by August 2002. In January 2000 a two-tier fare structure was introduced on buses within Greater London. A single journey involving travel in Zone 1 was charged at £1. Any journey wholly outside Zone 1 was 70p. Looking to the future this new fare structure is seen as a precursor to a universal single flat fare for all London bus travel, which would enable the devolpment of a simple smartcard stored-value ticket dispensed from a roadside ticket machine.

Appendix 2: Keeping Tabs

The past 40 years have witnessed the development of many novel systems designed to keep track of bus movements and position 'in the field'. The first was BESI (Bus Electronic Scanning Indicator). The idea was that each bus on specified routes would have its route and running number coded in a plate fixed to the side of the upper deck. As buses passed special scanners placed at intervals along the route, an electronic eye would read the code on the plate and pass the information to a central control room where it was transmitted onto a screen. Trials with BESI were begun late in 1957 on route 74 and by the mid-1960s BESI was helping to sort out delays on six busy routes including the 6, 9 and 13. However, traffic problems were such that BESI would have had to have been applied to a significant proportion of routes to be really effective and use of the system ceased in 1976. A small-scale experiment in 1972 with 2-way radios linking bus drivers and route controllers was followed in 1973 by CARLA (Computer Assisted Radio Location Aid) which was centred on route 11. With the help of a computer, a centrally based route controller could keep track of each bus by measuring wheel revolutions. CARLA was not very successful and experimentation had ended by 1976.

London Transport did not merely confine its efforts in solving traffic congestion to evaluating sophisticated computer-based systems. By 1976, 200 route inspectors had been issued with pocket radios and many buses had been fitted with radios too. The number had doubled by 1977, by which time 1,500 of LT's buses had been fitted with radios. Bus crews could thus be kept in contact with the central controllers to report unusual traffic conditions and other out-of-course events. The radios were fitted to every London bus by 1987.

By the mid-1980s trials were well under way on the 36 group of routes with BUSCO, another computerised weapon in the battle against traffic delays. BUSCO linked drivers and route controllers who had at their desks a visual display unit showing the scheduled and actual location of all buses on the route. Any gaps in service could thus be detected and remedial action taken. The lack of radio channels led BUSCO designers to use a system of standard coded messages transmitted to display screens fitted in bus cabs. The computer contacted each bus in turn to find out how far it had travelled since passing the last in a series of road loops; it then read any message from the drivers which they could send by pressing one of the function keys on a keyboard in the bus cab. The computer could also send messages to the driver.

Use of BUSCO has now been phased out, but an interesting by-product of it was PIBS (Passenger Information at Bus Stops). In trials conducted in the Lewisham and New Cross areas starting in August 1986, PIBS told waiting bus passengers what they always wanted to know: how long it would be before the next bus arrived. A screen attached inside the roofs of bus shelters displayed messages like '36B 2 and 7 minutes'.

In May 1992 London Transport unveiled Countdown, real-time passenger information along an entire route, in this case the 18 from Sudbury to King's Cross. Bus drivers enter bus destination details transmitted over radio link to microwave beacons. Wheel turn counters do the rest, sending details of the latest beacon to be passed, and the wheel count, over the radio to a central computer at Westbourne Park garage. The computer estimates time of arrival at each stop based on expected journey time and the speed of previous buses. Display panels at bus shelters show a three-line LED giving destination information and arrival times of the next three buses.

Countdown, which was in place at 1,000 bus stops by 2000, is part of a system called Fleetwide Automatic Vehicle Location (FAVL) which uses similar beacons to those providing the Countdown information to track the location of buses. Initially introduced on routes 28, 31 and 70, controlled from Westbourne Park, the system was gradually extended with the co-operation of many London bus route operators. By 2000 more than 3,000 buses were fitted with FAVL equipment enabling bus operators to control services at busy locations. The capabilities of FAVL also allowed experimentation with on-board dot-matrix displays on some bus routes, telling passengers the name of the next stop to be reached.

To assist in keeping buses on the move and running to time, a specialist sector within LT Buses, the Bus Priority and Traffic Unit, developed a number of important measures aimed, as the name of the unit suggested, at giving buses priority over other traffic. The unit worked in co-operation with the Traffic Director for London, Government Office for London, London Borough Councils and other bodies. Apart from a network of bus priority lanes along major trunk roads (Red Routes), plans were laid for a 500 mile London Bus Priority Network of bus lanes and other priority measures to cover 65 per cent of the locations which bus operators identified as being the worst traffic trouble spots. Implementation of the network began early in 1996, following successful trials in the Fulham and Shepherd's Bush areas, the Uxbridge Road and Docklands where delays were considerably reduced in the target areas.

Computer technology, in the form of Selective Vehicle Detection, also assisted service reliability by giving priority to the passage of buses across traffic light junctions. Transponders fitted to buses activated a loop buried in the road about 70 metres from a traffic light junction. These relayed the approach of the bus to the lights which then changed in favour of the bus. This system, called SCOOT, was part of a Europe-wide initiative and was first tried out in London in October 1994 at busy junctions in Camden Town and Edgware

A Countdown display, taking the uncertainty out of the wait for a bus.

Road. Another system, SPRINT (Selective Priority in Networks Technique), acts in the same way as SCOOT but within Urban Traffic Control Networks closely spaced sets of traffic lights are controlled centrally. By 2000 five hundred busy junctions had been fitted with traffic signal priority equipment allowing traffic signal timings to be regulated according to traffic conditions and giving buses the priority they need at peak times.

By the late 1990s the London Bus Priority Network was expanding at an impressive pace thanks to additional Government funding. At many busy junctions in central London as well as in suburban centres, buses had priority over other traffic. The next innovation is the London Bus Initiative, which will take in 27 routes and bring improvements to all elements of them, including speed, accessibility and comfort. Bus priority measures will include 'virtual' bus lanes on roads too narrow to accommodate a separate lane. The success of virtual bus lanes depends on the management of traffic queues to allow buses to keep moving.

Appendix 3: Night Buses

London's night bus services can be traced back to 1913 when the General introduced night route 94 from Cricklewood to Liverpool Street via Edgware Road, Oxford Street, Regent Street, Strand, Cannon Street, and Bank. There had been some all night tram services since 1901 but the 94, and its sister route the 94A which was introduced later in 1913, were London's very first night bus routes. They were suspended in 1916 because of wartime fuel shortages and did not reappear until 1920. Some night journeys were added to normal daytime routes in 1923 and thereafter the network grew, albeit slowly. By 1934 there were 12 night bus routes, almost all of them north of the Thames, night services in the south being the province of the trams which also continued to run on some north London routes until being replaced by trolleybuses in the late 1930s. Like their daytime contemporaries the night services have been altered down the years with journeys tailored to fit different requirements, largely night workers such as newspapermen and office cleaners, but the basic pattern of service remained unaltered for many

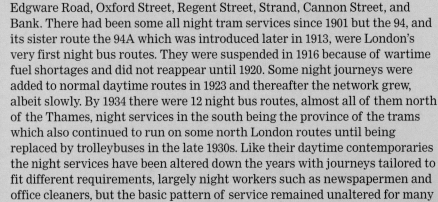

years until April 1984 when the whole network was enlarged for a growing leisure market. The new services proved popular, especially on Friday and Saturday nights when capacity problems were experienced on many of the routes out of central London. There have been frequent additions and alterations since.